Baseball's Greatest
Controversies

Also by John G. Robertson

The Babe Chases 60: That Fabulous 1927 Season, Home Run by Home Run (McFarland 1999; paperback 2014)

A's Bad as It Gets: Connie Mack's Pathetic Athletics of 1916 (McFarland 2014)

Baseball's Greatest Controversies

Rhubarbs, Hoaxes, Blown Calls, Ruthian Myths, Managers' Miscues and Front-Office Flops

John G. Robertson

McFarland & Company, Inc., Publishers
Jefferson, North Carolina

The present work is a reprint of the library bound edition of Baseball's Greatest Controversies: Rhubarbs, Hoaxes, Blown Calls, Ruthian Myths, Managers' Miscues and Front-Office Flops, *first published in 1995 by McFarland.*

LIBRARY OF CONGRESS CATALOGUING-IN-PUBLICATION DATA

Robertson, John G., 1964–
Baseball's greatest controversies : rhubarbs, hoaxes, blown calls, Ruthian myths, managers' miscues and front-office flops / John G. Robertson.
p. cm.
Includes bibliographical references and index.

ISBN 978-0-7864-9368-5
softcover : acid free paper ∞

1. Baseball—United States—History. 2. Baseball—United States—Anecdotes. I. Title.
GV863.A1R58 2014
796.357'0973—dc20 94-48265

BRITISH LIBRARY CATALOGUING DATA ARE AVAILABLE

Manufactured in the United States of America

McFarland & Company, Inc., Publishers
Box 611, Jefferson, North Carolina 28640
www.mcfarlandpub.com

This book is dedicated to the Babe Ruths of this world who got credit for something they didn't do, the Alexander Cartwrights of this world who didn't get credit for something they did do, the Fred Merkles of this world who did something that everybody else was doing but were vilified for it anyway, and the Sam Rices of this world who made us wonder what happened in the first place.

Contents

Introduction

To the naïve, baseball is an uncomplicated little game composed of four basic units: throwing the ball, hitting the ball, catching the ball, and running the bases. With such a simple premise, how many arguments and disputes could baseball possibly produce? The answer, of course, is "plenty."

What the uninitiated fail to realize is that baseball, behind its facade of pastoral simplicity, is a highly complex sport. The outcome of any particular game can often ride on subtleties which can produce sharp disagreement. Was the runner tagged out or did he manage to slide under the fielder's glove? Did the outfielder catch the ball or was it trapped? Did the runner actually touch the base or did he miss it by a fraction of an inch? Controversies such as these are endless. They make for lively discussion, but they normally have a limited lifespan.

But in the history of baseball, which goes back 150 years, some of the hottest disagreements have endured, still able to spark a fervent debate among scholars of the game. They are baseball's greatest controversies, and that is what this book is all about. Between its covers, this book will relive, rehash, discuss, analyze, and debate 25 of the game's most relished disputes. Perhaps a new generation of fans, unfamiliar with the Bob Feller–Phil Masi pickoff play in the 1948 World Series, will be able to get in on the debates and help perpetuate them.

The controversies this book deals with often go beyond what

took place on the playing fields in some of baseball's most important games. Some of them deal with myth, such as Babe Ruth's alleged "called shot" home run and Abner Doubleday's role in baseball's development. Others are more abstract. Did Harvey Haddix pitch a perfect game or not? Should Pete Rose have flattened Ray Fosse in the 1970 All-Star Game? Some controversies (like Fred Merkle's base-running blunder, which cost the New York Giants a trip to the World Series) border on the tragic, while others (like George Brett's "pine tar" home-run fiasco) are comical.

And what would baseball be without those magnificent feuds with umpires? The often anonymous arbiters of the game will have their most famous decision scrutinized again. Once you have finished reading this book, the names Don Denkinger, Larry Barnett, George Hildebrand, and Ken Burkhart will have as much significance as the names Babe Ruth, Ty Cobb, and Pete Rose. Well, almost as much.

I decided it would be best to present the controversies in chronological order. To attempt to list them in order of importance would be folly. It would be too arbitrary and would likely reflect personal bias. Fans of the 1985 St. Louis Cardinals might think that the chapter on Don Denkinger's erroneous call should come first. Other fans will have different opinions. The use of chronological order will enable me to escape the possibility of creating my own controversy.

Whether you are old enough to remember when the Yankees played their home games at the Polo Grounds or young enough to accept artificial turf as a natural part of the sport, *Baseball's Greatest Controversies* will either open up a flood of memories or enrich your knowledge of the game. Whatever the case, these 25 chapters will provide plenty of fuel to start a raging argument or two. After all, disputes have been part of baseball since Abner Doubleday laid out the first diamond, back in 1839. Or did he?

Chapter 1

The Hoax That Will Not Die: Cooperstown and the Doubleday Myth

> As far as anyone knows, he [Abner Doubleday] was as removed from the game as a Tibetan lama and didn't know a baseball from a kumquat.
>
> —Donald Honig in *Baseball America*

Let the record show that Abner Doubleday *did not* invent the grand old game of baseball. It would be far more appropriate and accurate to label Doubleday as the man whom baseball invented.

For the better part of a century, many baseball fans have been under the impression that Abner Doubleday, a graduate of West Point and a notable Union general in the Civil War, was solely responsible for outlining and originating America's national pastime, despite the overwhelming evidence that others have far more legitimate claims, and that Doubleday himself was nowhere near Cooperstown, New York, baseball's alleged birthplace, when this momentous event was supposed to have occurred. Any decent book dealing with baseball history published in the last 20 years will acknowledge this. But it is difficult to persuade those who would rather accept the neat and tidy Doubleday tale than believe that baseball's development is long, complex, and not necessarily rooted in the United States.

Baseball, of course, is loaded with myths. The stories of monumental home runs, fantastic catches, and other superhuman feats are sprinkled throughout the game's lore. Chapter 11 of this book delves into one of the game's most enduring myths, Babe Ruth's alleged "called shot" home run in the 1932 World Series. Stories such as this are relatively harmless. Does it really matter whether Ruth actually pointed to Wrigley Field's center-field seats before launching a mammoth home run off of Cubs pitcher Charlie Root? Not really. Ruth indeed hit a home run; you could look it up, as Casey Stengel used to say. The controversy behind whether he pointed or not does not change the fact that a home run was hit by Ruth during that particular at-bat. If anything, the exaggerated stories that have circulated since that Saturday afternoon six decades ago have enhanced the sport and given it a certain majesty that separates baseball from all of the other athletic diversions in America. There is truly no harm in the story, whether one is inclined to believe it or not.

There is, however, much maliciousness in the farfetched and ludicrous claim that Abner Doubleday, according to a group of "investigators" known as the Mills Commission, scratched out his idea for a new sport called "base ball" in a vacant lot in Cooperstown in the summer of 1839. The report filed by the commission was deliberately designed to ignore the contributions made by others and was part of a grand scheme to market the sport as a true-blue, all–American game without any evil, foreign influences.

Nobody was very much concerned with where or how baseball developed until Henry Chadwick had the audacity to state the obvious and voice his opinion that baseball had decidedly British origins, springing from traditional English games of rounders and cricket. Chadwick had impeccable credentials, being one of the sport's earliest historians and record keepers (his work would earn him a place in the Hall of Fame for meritorious service). The truth of Chadwick's statements, which came at the end of the nineteenth century, did not sit well with some members of the baseball hierarchy. America, they said, was a fully independent nation whose culture and values were completely separate from any European influence. Didn't it stand to reason that baseball should reflect this American ideal of independent growth? Baseball must certainly be a purely American game. Those who strongly felt this way were bound and determined to prove it, and the Mills Commission was born.

The commission itself was formed at the request of Albert Spalding, who founded the famous sporting-goods company which bears his name. As members of this panel, Spalding summoned A. G. Mills (described as "an enthusiastic ball player before and during the Civil War"), who was the National League's third president; Arthur P. Gorman, a senator from Maryland; Morgan G. Bulkeley, the first president of the National League and a former governor of Connecticut; and four other men of high repute. They held their first meeting in 1905, stating that their mandate was to determine, once and for all, the origins of baseball. Two years later, after accumulating what was described as "the best available evidence," the commission reported that baseball was an American game and that it had been invented by Abner Doubleday, in the general's hometown of Cooperstown in 1839, while he was on leave from his studies at the United States Military Academy.

This conclusion fully satisfied the nationalists who were adamant that baseball had to have been invented in America. Hooray! Baseball was indeed the national game, and Spalding could unashamedly promote his line of sporting apparel as representing the height of patriotism. The end result was the intended result, and few bothered to question the Mills Commission about how it had arrived at this convenient conclusion. But it was a legitimate question, and latter-day historians have been considerably more inquiring and skeptical than Spalding and his friends were back in 1907.

The Mills Commission's findings were largely forgotten until the 1930s, when the Great Depression began to hurt baseball attendance at all levels of the game. Grasping for the ideas to regenerate interest and excitement into the sport, Baseball Commissioner Kenesaw Mountain Landis resurrected the dust-covered Mills report, which indicated that baseball's centennial was close at hand. Could there be a better promotional gimmick than this? Landis and his contemporaries intended to milk this notion for all it was worth.

Why not establish a national baseball museum in Cooperstown? How about a Hall of Fame to honor great baseball figures of the past? By the mid–1930s, with the Depression at its worst, Landis foisted his plan upon the gullible public, who eagerly embraced the idea. Elections were held, the museum was built, and artifacts from the game began to trickle in. But some people began to wonder about the credibility of the Doubleday/Cooperstown story. How truthful was it? The answer, it turns out, is "not very."

It seems that the Mills Commission, much like the Warren Commission, which investigated the assassination of President Kennedy 60 years later, had defined what they wanted their answer to be before the investigation had even begun. Disregarding evidence that ancient Egyptians had played games with a ball and bat five thousand years earlier, disregarding evidence that "base ball" had figured in a children's rhyme book in England in 1744, disregarding written and pictorial accounts of baseball-like contests in colonial America, disregarding all of that and more, the Mills Commission opted to base their entire decision on a letter from an elderly man named Abner Graves who "remembered" his boyhood pal, Abner Doubleday, explaining his idea for a new game called baseball. Graves' letter stated that Doubleday outlined his basic ideas to him and measured out the first diamond in one of Cooperstown's vacant lots. This bit of hearsay evidence alone was apparently enough to satisfy the Mills Commission, as no other evidence ever surfaced to back up the claim that Doubleday was indeed the father of baseball.

Unfortunately for those who religiously accept the Doubleday myth, Graves' story had more holes in it than the St. Louis Browns' defense. First of all, Doubleday was a cadet at West Point in the summer of 1839 and there is no record of his being absent from the academy at that time. Secondly, Graves was barely five years old at the time, while Doubleday was almost 20. Furthermore, even if Doubleday had left West Point on leave that summer, he had no reason to go to Cooperstown. His family had moved away from there two years earlier. Of course, Doubleday could not be summoned to refute these silly claims. He had died in 1893, some 14 years before the Mills Commission proclaimed him as a major historical sports figure.

Doubleday was a very meticulous man. Apparently his training at West Point had taught him to keep punctual and accurate records of his thoughts and actions. When he died, he left behind 67 books which comprised his diary. The word "baseball" does not appear in any of those volumes. Not even once. This should sufficiently demonstrate that Doubleday did not start baseball. (Some military historians claim he started something even bigger: the Civil War! Apparently, Doubleday fired the first Union cannon blast from Fort Sumter.)

The truth of the matter is that baseball did not enjoy a neat, swift birth. The English had been playing cricket and rounders since the thirteenth century, and various bat-and-ball games had evolved from them. "Town ball," "the Boston game," and other derivatives were practiced in colonial America. Woodcuts and other pictorial evidence of these contests were available to the members of the Mills Commission, if they had taken the time to properly pursue their mandate. Crude forms of baseball had been popping up all over the New World for two centuries. (Some stuffy town elders apparently disapproved of such folly. The civil leaders of Cooperstown had passed a bylaw prohibiting "ball playing" within the city limits as early as 1819-20 years before Doubleday was said to have invented the game in his fertile mind!)

Despite the proliferation of these games, they were a far cry from modern baseball. Stakes and spikes were the earliest forms of bases. And those who actually dared to run the bases could be impeded by infielders who were permitted to trip and tackle them! Even worse, some games' rules declared that the only way to retire runners was to "soak them," meaning to hit them with a thrown ball. Such rough and uncivilized games were probably doomed to extinction, unless someone came forth to clean them up, establish standardized rules, and promote the game as wholesome recreation. Luckily for baseball, such a man emerged. His name was Alexander Joy Cartwright, and it is he who should be honored as the true father of modern baseball, rather than Abner Doubleday.

Cartwright, a New Jersey engineer and an avid sportsman, was troubled by the roughness which plagued ball games, and dedicated his time to establishing a more palatable sport. Records indicate that by 1845 Cartwright had written a code of rules which declared that teams would consist of nine players each, bases would be 90 feet apart, and lines would be drawn on the field to determine fair and foul balls. Runners would now be put out by tagging or touching the base ahead of them. Three outs would end an inning. Cartwright had laid the foundations for the game which would quickly become America's pastime and passion.

June 19, 1846, was the first important date in baseball history. On that date, in a recreational area of Hoboken, New Jersey, known as the Elysian Fields, the Cartwright rules were first used in an organized game, and baseball was born. Oddly enough, Cartwright's team, the Knickerbocker Club, was defeated 23–1 by the New York Club in four innings. (According to the original Cartwright rules, a game was over once one team scored 21 runs or "aces" and each team had had the same number of turns at bat. Some cynical observers believe that Cartwright's team may have deliberately dumped the first-ever game to the New York team in order to generate enthusiasm for the sport in their opponents.) Baseball was on its way, and soon became a fashionable diversion in high society. Gentlemen of distinction took their whacks at the plate in a game that more closely resembled today's slow-pitch softball than modern baseball. The Civil War saw the game played as a recreational activity in army camps of both the South and the North, introducing it to many soldiers who had been unaware of the sport's existence.

There was no stopping baseball now. By 1869, the Cincinnati Red Stockings had professional players, proving that gentlemen of leisure didn't always make the best athletes. As a touring team in their first season, the Red Stockings went undefeated and often played before large, boisterous crowds. In 1871, the first all-professional league, the National Association, was founded, and survived five rocky seasons. In 1876, a couple of months before General Custer charged into the Sioux at the Little Bighorn, the National League opened its first season. By this time, baseball was being played in every state in the union, not to mention in Canada and in exotic locales such as Hawaii and Japan.

The evidence is absolutely irrefutable. Cartwright was the founder of modern baseball, not Doubleday. Hoboken, New Jersey, is its rightful birthplace, not Cooperstown, New York. Still, if one walks down the tree-lined streets of Cooperstown, passes by the stores, churches, and parks, one is almost forced to think that if baseball wasn't invented here, it probably should have been.

Chapter 2

1904: The First Year Without a World Series

> It is almost impossible to picture baseball without this spectacular climax to the season, for what good would the pennant races be if the goal were not a place in the World Series? Certainly, baseball minus a World Series would lose its vibrancy.
>
> —Joseph L. Reichler in *The World Series*

Before the unthinkable happened in 1994, the concept of the major-league baseball season not ending with the World Series was completely foreign to most fans. For most of the twentieth century, the champions of the National and American leagues had battled it out each autumn for unquestioned supremacy. The World Series has been a mainstay of the sporting scene and an indelible part of American culture. October is synonymous with baseball's premier event. Not having it in 1994 left a void in most fans' sporting calendar. Baseball fans who have not been schooled in the sport's colorful and illustrious history would find it hard to believe that at one time major-league baseball managed to survive and flourish without an annual postseason tilt. In fact, there were those vehemently opposed to the whole idea of a series to determine the true champions of major-league baseball. Moreover, once the precedent had been set, and the first modern World Series had been played in October of

1903, some men with clout—most notably John McGraw, the New York Giants' manager, and John T. Brush, the club's owner—were so appalled by the idea that they alone quashed the 1904 World Series. Look it up in the record books. No World Series was played that year, the only such absence from 1903 to 1993.

Ask a history student what the year 1876 means, and a few answers are bound to emerge. Rutherford B. Hayes was elected to the presidency of the United States by the slimmest of margins. Alexander Graham Bell demonstrated the practical use of the telephone. General George Armstrong Custer came out the loser when he underestimated the strength of the Sioux. A history student with a passion for baseball, however, might supply one further answer: The National League was founded, giving birth to major-league baseball.

Of course, 1876 was not the year the sport was born. The game as we know it had been regularly played since 1846 and was quickly growing into the national sport of America. Amateur clubs sprang up at a huge rate, travelling professional teams were formed, and the game was on solid footing. All that was missing was a major professional league dedicated to a high quality of play on the field and, more important, strong leadership in its administration. The first major pro league was the National Association, which played five erratic seasons from 1871 to 1875. Scheduling was haphazard, record keeping was spotty, and lax regulations doomed it. When the league called it quits after 1875, concerned baseball men gathered to pick up the pieces. They discussed the faults of the dearly departed National Association and agreed to form a new league, one which would be dedicated to preserving the dignity of the game. Rules were going to be strictly enforced. Teams would play their games on the scheduled dates—or else. The new loop was called the National League of Professional Baseball Clubs. It began play in April of 1876, two months before Custer fatally erred at the Little Bighorn.

With a standard admission fee of 50 cents per head (rather steep, considering that a newspaper could be purchased for a penny), the National League got through its first season. Chicago won the championship, having accumulated the best regular-season record. There was no playoff; as far as the spectators were concerned, it wasn't needed. In what was probably its toughest and wisest move, the directors of the NL severely punished the New York and Philadelphia clubs—they were, in fact, booted out of the league—for refusing to make late-season road trips when the pennant was beyond their reach. The move was a statement that no individual club was above the league as a whole. The National League had stood behind its principles and was applauded for making its member clubs accountable to the public.

The NL operated as a monopoly through the 1881 season. Some clubs came and went, but the league remained financially solvent and became established as a fixture in the minds of America's baseball fans. The sport came in for some drastic changes starting in 1882. That season, the American Association, known to the self-righteous National League owners as "the beer league" because it allowed the sale of liquor at its ballparks, opened up for business to try to break the NL's iron grip on the professional game. By 1884, a third pro circuit, called the Union Association, bankrolled almost entirely by millionaire Henry V. Lucas, established clubs in cities large and small in a similar attempt to lure paying customers away from the turnstiles of National League parks. With two and sometimes three games going on simultaneously in the same city, the overall results were catastrophic. Attendance in all three leagues was abysmal. Often, fewer than a hundred souls were present in the grandstands. The Union Association, not as well organized as the AA or the NL, packed it in after one year and is only remembered by the heartiest of baseball fans today. Both the NL and the AA accepted their losses, but refused to merge. However, in 1884 both leagues agreed to have their respective champions play an annual "world's championship series" as a way to recoup their financial losses and regenerate waning fan interest. These series were sometimes a joke, with squabbles and on-field controversies further tarnishing the fragile state of the sport. For example, the winner of the 1885 series in still in dispute because of a forfeited game recognized by one league but not the other. Fan interest never truly peaked with this yearly postseason event, and when the American Association relinquished its major-league status after the 1891 season, there were few fans who lamented the loss of the original World Series.

The National League was on its own for another decade. The season ended, as far as most fans were concerned, with the final games on the schedule. A postseason series known as the Temple Cup, between the two clubs which finished first and second in the NL, was attempted for a few seasons in the 1890s. Few fans attended, however, so the Temple Cup, a gaudy piece of silver, was relegated to history, and later to a display case in Cooperstown.

Another rival outfit, the American League, was formed by Ban Johnson in 1900. Springing from the Western League, Johnson's circuit was his answer to the NL's obnoxious monopoly of the national sport. He believed the public would see the AL as a positive alternative. Beginning in 1901, Johnson's league raided the NL clubs' rosters and persuaded some of its biggest stars to jump to the new league. The fans responded, too, many drawn by the cheaper AL admission rate of 25 cents. Since Johnson strategically placed franchises in most of the NL cities, the longtime owners of the NL clubs were dismayed by what they considered to be acts of piracy orchestrated by their competition. Despite dire predictions that the AL would end up bankrupt and fall apart (the fate which had befallen the Union Association in 1884), the new league survived and won a great deal of fan support. AL games started on time, the players displayed hustle, and the owners were actually civil in their dealings with the public. To the horror of the NL owners, Ban Johnson's experiment succeeded. The AL was here to stay.

The NL owners accepted this reality only grudgingly. They agreed to meet with the AL owners to devise schedules so that, wherever possible, two big league games wouldn't be going on in the same city at the same time. But that was about the extent of the cooperation. To some NL men, their circuit was still the only true major league, while the AL was merely a group of upstarts who were sabotaging their business interests. The AL played its first season in 1901. A second season the following year proved that the new league was in no immediate danger of folding. Another solid season in 1903 confirmed that two major leagues could operate side by side and generate enough profits for all concerned. The owner of the NL club in Pittsburgh was Barney Dreyfuss, an open-minded businessman who sensed that the public would warm to a championship series between the two leagues. He came up with what was considered a radical idea near the end of the 1903 season.

When it appeared that his club would take the NL pennant and the Boston AL club would win that league's title, Dreyfuss penned a letter to Boston owner Henry Killilea. Quoted in *The World Series*, it said, in part:

> The time has come for the National League and the American League to organize a World Series. It is my belief that if our clubs played a series on a best-of-nine basis, we would create great interest in baseball, in our leagues, and in our players. I also believe it would be a financial success.

After discussing Dreyfuss' proposal with AL president Ban Johnson, Killilea agreed to participate in the postseason clash with the NL champions. One of the great sporting spectacles, the World Series, was born. To the shock of many who were under the impression that the NL was still the epitome of fine baseball, the AL champions from Boston won the initial World Series with Pittsburgh by five games to three. Despite the tremendous crowds which attended each game, many NL owners were horrified by the series. Barney Dreyfuss' actions had legitimized the American League! The National League could no longer claim to be the nation's premier baseball circuit by reputation alone. Pittsburgh's embarrassing loss had greatly damaged the prestige of the NL and something had to be done to restore it. The events of 1904 would provide two villains who would perpetrate an act which most baseball fans found totally unpalatable. They would attempt to kill the World Series.

The 1904 season was a laugher for the NL's New York Giants. By midsummer it was apparent that the Giants would end the Pittsburgh Pirates' three-year grip on the NL pennant. Blessed with the great pitching of legendary Christy Mathewson and Joe McGinnity, John McGraw's club made a joke of the pennant race. The Giants finished the NL schedule with a fine record of 106 wins against just 47 losses, 13 games in front of second-place Chicago. The Giants' owner, John T. Brush, while happy with his team's success on the field, was less than thrilled with what was occurring in the AL. New York's entry in the AL (known at the time as the Greater New

Yorks; the nickname Yankees wouldn't come for another decade) was involved in a terrific three-team pennant race, and was outdrawing the Giants at the gate. Fans had conceded the NL flag to the Giants and had little reason to spend their money to watch Brush's team. Instead, large crowds, sometimes approaching the fantastic total of thirty thousand, were attending American League games in New York City. Worse yet for Brush was the fact that the Greater New Yorks were likely to win their league's pennant. This outcome would mean that the Giants could not even claim to be the best baseball team in their own city unless Brush consented to play his rivals in a series. He had no such plans to put his mighty Giants to the test against the upstarts from the AL—especially if the opponents happened to be the Greater New Yorks. Giants manager John McGraw wasn't exactly chomping at the bit to engage in a postseason series with any AL club. He had a simmering personal feud with Ban Johnson. McGraw had had a brief but stormy managerial career in the AL in which he had run afoul of Johnson's heavy-handed leadership. Johnson disliked McGraw intensely, and was appalled by the manner in which McGraw berated AL umpires. Finally, partway through the 1902 season, Johnson surpassed his patience with the fiery McGraw, and turfed him out of the league, much to the relief of the AL's beleaguered men in blue.

Therefore, for entirely different reasons, neither McGraw not Brush had any desire to play a World Series. Joseph Gordon, who owned New York's AL club, nevertheless took it upon himself to write a letter to Brush asking his club to play the Greater New Yorks if both teams happened to win their respective pennants. Gordon distributed copies of the letter to the New York press. Quoted in *The New York Times*, it said,

> On behalf of the Greater New York Baseball Club of the American League, I hereby challenge the New York National League Club to play a series of seven games for the world's championship in the event of the winning of the American League pennant by the Greater New Yorks. In view of the general popular demand, and in the interest of true sportsmanship, I believe such a series should be arranged forthwith.

> The New York public, which has supported the game loyally through years of vicissitudes, is entitled to consideration, and the time has arrived, in my estimation, when this support should be rewarded by the playing of a series which will be memorable in baseball history.

No dice, said both Brush and McGraw. McGraw, in a pompous statement, declared that there was nothing in the NL's constitution which required the NL champions to play a series against the champions of "a minor league." As far as Brush and McGraw were concerned, the winning of the NL pennant made the Giants undisputed world champions.

As it turned out, Brush's club would not have had to play the Greater New Yorks, who blew the pennant to the Boston AL club in the final week of the season. The telling blow came when 41-game winner Jack Chesbro unleashed a wild pitch in the first game of a season-ending doubleheader against the Boston Pilgrims. The errant toss allowed Boston to score the winning run in a 3–2 victory, clinching the city's second straight AL flag.

Still, the fans were outraged. They wanted to see a Boston–New York clash for all the marbles. When no series was forthcoming, irate fans criticized Brush and McGraw and vowed to boycott both AL and NL games unless a postseason series became an annual ritual. Brush, who had made his fortune in the department-store business and should have gauged public sentiment better than he did, admitted his refusal to play the AL champions was selfish, shortsighted, and irresponsible. Both leagues made arrangements for a World Series to be played at the conclusion of each season beginning in 1905. It was a happy tradition which ran uninterrupted until the aborted 1994 season.

Fans who wanted to see McGraw's Giants punished for the acts perpetrated by the club's manager and owner in 1904 did not get their wish. The Giants repeated as NL champions in 1905, and drubbed the AL champions from Philadelphia four games to one in the subsequent World Series.

Chapter 3

"Bonehead Merkle": The Baserunning Blunder That Lost a Pennant (1908)

> A run is not scored if the runner advances to home base during a play in which the third out is made by any runner being forced out.
>
> —*The Official Rules of Baseball*, Rule 4.09 (a)

Fred Merkle was probably not unlike thousands of ballplayers who have picked up a ball, a bat, a glove, or a pair of spikes since the sport became forever part of the fabric of American society a century ago. Merkle was more talented than most, of course. He had a long and successful career in the major leagues at a time when minor-league baseball was flourishing and many hopefuls could only dream of playing baseball at the major league level. Merkle, though, was very much like his counterparts at all levels of the game in one respect: he had never bothered to read a rule book, much less consider the consequences of routine actions (or inactions) which occur with monotonous regularity in each game. Therefore, it is relatively safe to assume that Fred Merkle had never heard of Rule 4.09 (a) until one fateful September day in 1908 when this one sentence from baseball's bible emerged to haunt him. It is also safe to assume that Merkle never forgot the implications of Rule 4.09 (a) after that day until his death in 1956.

One of the reasons why baseball has such an enduring appeal to its fans is that the game has changed very little in the years since the turn of the century. While other sports, such as basketball or football, have undergone drastic changes in the last four or five decades, baseball has remained a model of consistency. The bases are still 90 feet apart, as they were when Ty Cobb was circling them. The pitching rubber is still 60 feet 6 inches from the back point of home plate, just as it was when Walter Johnson and Rube Waddell were frustrating batters with their fastballs. Baseball's scoring rules, a difficult-to-read collection of whereases and therefores, have also remained very much intact throughout the sport's glorious history. Most spectators and players acquire their knowledge of these foundations of the game through observation, discussion, and experience. It would be absurd to even imagine a Little League manager addressing his ten-year-olds during practice and saying, "Today we're going to discuss how we might imperil our team's chances of victory if we fail to abide by Rule 4.09 (a)!" Most players will admit they are exposed to rules interpretations only through hearsay and cruel experience. And nobody ever had a crueler experience with baserunning rules than Fred Merkle.

Before rehashing the grim details of Fred Merkle's casual baserunning blunder, let's examine how Rule 4.09 (a) works by studying two typical situations. Situation #1: Bases loaded and two out. Batter hits a sharp ground ball to the second baseman, who bobbles it. The runner stationed on first base is slow, the runner on third base is a jackrabbit. The second baseman eventually gets control of the ball and throws to his shortstop, who is covering second base. The shortstop catches the throw and steps on second to retire the lumbering runner coming from first. However, the fleet runner from third had already crossed the plate before his teammate was put out. Does this run count? The answer is an emphatic "No!" Why not? Just look at 4.09 (a). Since the third out came on a force play (i.e., the runner at first was forced to advance as soon as the batter hit a fair ground ball), no run can score, regardless of how fast the lead runner happens to be. It's a play that occurs dozens of times during a baseball season on every major league club. No one even bothers to question the logic behind it; it is a standard inning-ending play.

Now try Situation #2. Runner on third base with two out. Batter hits a single into right field. Runner on third crosses the plate. Batter tries to stretch his single into a double, but is thrown out at second base for the third out. Does the run count here? Absolutely! Since the third out was not on a force play (i.e., the runner tried to advance to second without being forced to by a subsequent runner), we have what is called a timing play. The umpires must determine what happened first to decide whether or not the run should count. Since the runner clearly scored before the third out was made, the run would count.

The force play and the timing play are the foundation of all baseball scoring rules. When something peculiar happens during the course of the game, they are what good umpiring crews must rely upon. They supersede common practice, and some would say they also overruled common sense in the case of Fred Merkle.

The early autumn of 1908 should have been a wonderful time in the life of young Fred Merkle. A couple of months shy of his twentieth birthday, Merkle was a rookie on John McGraw's New York Giants baseball club, arguably the world's most famous team. New York City was absolutely mad about baseball, and devoted readers of *The Sporting News* were enthralled by fascinating pennant races in both major leagues. Detroit, Cleveland, and Chicago were locked in a ferocious three-way race for the American League flag, a race that the Tigers would win by the slimmest of margins—one-half game over Cleveland. Although the National League could not match the intensity of three clubs vying for the pennant, the NL race was being fought just as fiercely between the defending champion Chicago Cubs and the rejuvenated New York Giants, who were attempting to regain their championship form of 1905, the season when they defeated the Philadelphia Athletics in five games in the World Series without allowing an earned run.

Both the Cubs and the Giants were loaded with talent. Chicago could boast of the sparkling defense of their infielders. The double-play combination of shortstop Joe Tinker, second baseman Johnny Evers, and first baseman Frank Chance was the stuff of legends. (It would be the stuff of poets too, as Franklin P. Adams would link the three forever in his famous work *Baseball's Sad Lexicon.*) Mordecai "Three Finger" Brown won 29 games for Chicago. Ed Reulbach won 24. The Giants' superstar was pitching ace Christy Mathewson, whose statistics must seem mind-boggling to modern-day hurlers. Mathewson pitched 391 innings, had a 37–11 won-lost record, and an earned-run average of 1.43. Mathewson also led the league with 259 strikeouts, 60 more than his closest rival. He also tied for the NL lead in saves with five, when relief pitching was an oddity. The Giants' right fielder, Mike Donlin, was the club's major offensive threat, with a batting average of .334 (second only to Honus Wagner). Donlin also finished in the top five in five other offensive categories, including hits, home runs, and runs batted in. With so much firepower in both lineups, it seems incredible that the fate of the 1908 NL pennant would come down to the feet of a rookie from Watertown, Wisconsin, named Fred Merkle who had yet to appear in 60 big league games.

Wednesday, September 23, 1908, was an exciting afternoon for the thousands of New York baseball fans who crowded into the Polo Grounds to root for their beloved Giants. A festive air filled the stands; the locals were confident that the home side could defeat the visiting Chicago Cubs and take control of the National League pennant race. No one present had any idea that they were about to witness one of baseball's most infamous baserunning debacles and a pennant race thrown into confusion.

Things were looking extremely positive for the Giants in the bottom of the ninth inning. With the score tied 1–1, the Giants had put together a potentially game-winning rally. Two were out, but the Giants had two runners on base. Big Moose McCormick was stationed at third and young Fred Merkle was hugging the bag at first. The noise level grew considerably as Al Bridwell entered the batter's box. A hit now would lift the Giants to victory and put them in charge of the pennant chase. Bridwell did not disappoint the faithful, as he ripped a solid single into center field to score McCormick. McCormick hustled down the baseline, touched the plate, and headed to the clubhouse to escape the well-wishers who were invading the field. Merkle, seeing McCormick score the apparent winning run, did what 90 percent of ballplayers at that time would have done—he ran part of the distance toward second base, and then retreated toward the clubhouse *without bothering to touch second base*! Ordinarily, this would not have presented a problem for the Giants. However, on this particular day, one of their opponents was Johnny Evers, a man who had peculiar reading habits. While traveling on his club's train trips or resting in his hotel room, Evers liked to leaf through the baseball rule book. Most of his teammates were puzzled and amused by Evers, but his knowledge and insight into rules, particularly 4.09 (a), would pay great dividends today.

Evers had been waiting for such a situation to arise, and had actually tried to act on the same scenario once before. Earlier in the 1908 season, in a game in Pittsburgh, Evers noticed a Pirate runner neglect to touch second base in exactly the same circumstances. On that day, Evers retrieved the ball, stepped on second base, and appealed to base umpire Hank O'Day to call the runner out on a force play and nullify the run. O'Day thought about it for a moment before denying the out. He informed Evers that such a baserunning lapse was common practice and ought not to be penalized. Evers noted that the force was still on at second, regardless of what was considered common practice. Umpire O'Day still refused to grant the Cubs an out—but the seeds of doubt had been planted in his mind.

Evers realized at once that Merkle had erred in the very same manner as the earlier Pittsburgh runner. He frantically screamed for a teammate to relay the ball to him to make a force play at second base. Amid the chaos of celebrating fans, the Chicago outfielders tried to bring the ball back to Evers. Meanwhile, in the New York dugout, Giants pitcher Joe McGinnity sensed something was amiss. He ran onto the field, wrestled the ball away from the confused Cub outfielders, and threw it into the seats! There are conflicting reports about what happened next. Some witnesses say the Cubs threw a ball from their dugout onto the field. Others say a ball was grabbed from the umpire's bag. Whatever the case, Johnny Evers ended up with the ball and stepped on second base. By an amazing twist of fate, the base umpire that afternoon was Hank O'Day. Without hesitation, O'Day ruled Merkle out on a force play. McCormick's run was nullified and the game remained tied at 1–1.

Within moments of O'Day's decision, the happy, celebrating fans on the field turned into an angry mob. The Giants stormed the field, demanding to know why O'Day had ruled Merkle out. Simple, said O'Day, check Rule 4.09 (a). With the mob still roving in the field and darkness settling onto the Polo Grounds, the umpires decided to call the game at that point. According to league rules, the tie game would have to be replayed in its entirety at the end of the season if it had any bearing on the final standings. As it turned out, it had all the bearing on the final standings: the Cubs and Giants finished tied for first with 98–55 records. The game was replayed. The Cubs won 4–2 and captured their second straight National League pennant.

With emotions running high in New York, this was obviously a story that would not go away. One New York paper took to calling Merkle "Bonehead," despite the fact that other runners before him had neglected to touch second base in similar situations. Many writers felt that the Giants were the victims of a gigantic swindle. Despite the fact that Giants manager John McGraw never faulted Merkle, the young rookie could never escape the taunts of "Bonehead Merkle!" that always greeted him.

Many writers and historians have been quick to criticize umpire O'Day's out call in the ensuing years, but it was clearly correct according to the rules of the game. Few historians have given credit to Evers, who had the intelligence to recognize the opportunity to snatch victory from defeat. It is doubtful whether there has ever been a more appropriate "heads up" play in the history of major league baseball.

This story has a few postscripts. First, the Cubs made the most of their new life by knocking off Detroit in the World Series in five uneventful games. Second, the furor over O'Day's verdict prompted the Giants to file a protest to NL president Harry Pulliam. Pulliam upheld the umpire's call and became the target of angry New York sports writers. Upset and disillusioned, Pulliam committed suicide in July 1909.

Finally, what became of Fred Merkle? Even though he had every reason to distance himself from baseball, Merkle endured in the majors. He eventually played on six pennant winners, but never on a club that won a World Series. (Perhaps 1908 was his best chance!) He finished his career with 1,580 hits and a respectable batting average of .273. When his playing career finally ended, he decided to pursue a career in managing. One day in 1929, while piloting a Class D team in Daytona, Florida, he stormed off the field, never to return. Why? One of his youthful players had called him "Bonehead." As *The Baseball Hall of Shame* noted, near the end of his life Merkle lamented, "When I die, I guess they'll put on my tombstone, 'Here lies Bonehead Merkle.'"

They didn't.

Chapter 4

Cobb or Lajoie: Who Really Won the 1910 American League Batting Title?

> Ty [Cobb] had at one time or another spiked [his opponents], run them down, slugged them, bedeviled them, insulted them, intimidated them, humiliated them, or otherwise unsettled their digestive tracts.
>
> Napoleon [Lajoie] certainly did not lack acclaim nor fall short of idolators; in his heyday he was one of the most admired of baseball players. . ."
>
> —Donald Honig in *Baseball America*

It is difficult to believe, but a batting championship in the major leagues was once reduced to a popularity contest under circumstances which could either be described as comical or appalling, depending upon one's point of view. Batting championships, by nature, are purely statistical contests. Numbers don't lie, and the scoresheet doesn't know a jackass from an angel, so it would seem impossible for a batting title to become as subjective as, say, the voting for Gold Gloves or league MVP honors. Nevertheless, late in the 1910 season, the American League's batting championship more or less hinged on the fact that Ty Cobb was an irascible firebrand who alienated everybody in baseball (including his teammates and manager) while Napoleon Lajoie did not have an enemy in the world.

There are few surviving fans who can still give eyewitness testimony about the passionate way in which Tyrus Raymond Cobb played baseball. His unmatched competitive spirit bordered on the psychotic, and he drove himself to excel every time he stepped between the lines of a ball diamond. If one looks at his accomplishments (a lifetime batting average of .367, 12 American League batting championships, 892 stolen bases) the statistics alone can lead one to believe that Cobb was the greatest player ever to grace a lineup card. Yet cold statistics do not adequately sum up how Cobb played the game. Every inning, every pitch was a personal challenge to Cobb, who unleashed his fury over 24 seasons in a way that has never been duplicated. "Don't get Mr. Cobb angry," was the advice that Connie Mack passed along to his Philadelphia Athletics before they took the field in any game against Cobb's Detroit Tigers. Mack had good reason to say this. He knew that Cobb was a fierce enough competitor when in a reasonably pacific mood, but he was a fearsome animal if agitated, even in the slightest way.

One story which perhaps best illustrates how feared Cobb was by his opponents involves a pitcher for the Boston Red Sox named Cy Morgan. During a game in 1909, Cobb was convinced that Morgan was deliberately trying to hit him with fastballs. At one point in the game, Cobb was standing on second base when Morgan unleashed a wild pitch which eluded the catcher and hit the backstop. Cobb ran to third base, but had no intention of stopping there. He knew that Morgan would be covering home plate and Cobb intended to knock Morgan into the next county. The catcher retrieved the ball and threw it to Morgan at home. By this time Cobb was only a few feet past third base, but continued to charge toward the plate and Morgan. Instead of being glad for what was going to be an easy putout, Morgan saw the angry expression on Cobb's face and ran away from the plate! Cobb, needless to say, scored easily, and Morgan was traded to Philadelphia shortly thereafter.

Cobb didn't target his animosity only at opponents. Even his teammates found out early that they were not immune from Cobb's wrath. In his first season in the majors, Cobb severely beat his roommate. Why? The roommate had committed the high crime of showering before young Tyrus. No one could escape Cobb's irrational acts and fiery temper. During his career, Cobb assaulted an elevator operator, at least one waiter, and, in his most famous explosion, Cobb pummeled a crippled heckler in New York named Claude Luecker. When Cobb leapt into the stands to confront Luecker, teammates and other spectators tried to talk Cobb out of assaulting the man. "Don't hit him, Ty! He's got no hands!" pleaded an onlooker. "I don't care if he's got no feet!" replied Cobb, who proceeded to pound Luecker unmercifully until a squad of police officers pulled him away. It was little wonder why Cobb had few friends in the American League.

In direct contrast to Cobb was Napoleon "Larry" Lajoie, an affable man of French-Canadian descent who was often held up by the promoters of baseball as the perfect gentleman-athlete. Lajoie broke into the majors with the Philadelphia Phillies in 1896, and in his five seasons in the National League, he never batted below .324. His swing had a natural grace that belied the power behind it. Contemporaries declared that the sound of Lajoie's bat hitting a pitched ball had a distinct crack which could not be duplicated by any other player. The ball seemed to jump faster off Lajoie's bat, too. Infielders had to be especially alert when Lajoie was at the plate. The thought of being struck by a Lajoie line drive was simply scary, and it wasn't uncommon for the defense to play back a few feet in order to give their reflexes another split second to react to the rockets Lajoie regularly sent toward them.

When the 1901 season began, Phillies fans were surprised to learn that their favorite player, Lajoie, tired of receiving the pitiful paychecks which National League players were accustomed to, had jumped to the new major baseball circuit, the American League. The good news for the Philadelphia faithful was that Lajoie would be playing for Connie Mack's Athletics, the city's American League entry. And what a season he had! Lajoie proved to everyone that he was indeed the new league's supreme player. He batted .422 (still an AL record), drove in 125 runs, and banged out 14 homers to capture the triple crown. The figures are somewhat misleading, however. Foul balls did not count as strikes in the American League (that would change by 1903) and the overall talent in the AL certainly was not as deep as in the more established NL. But still, 1901 was a tremendous season for Lajoie, who was at the peak of a career which would lead him to Cooperstown.

The fans of the Athletics must have been livid in June of 1902 when Mack, always conscious of the ledger sheet, sold Lajoie's contract to Cleveland. The change in scenery didn't seem to hurt Lajoie's batting eye much. He won the AL batting title for his new club in both 1903 and 1904. For a while he *was* the franchise in Cleveland. So revered was he by the fans and reporters that the Cleveland club was, more often than not, referred to as the Naps, indicating that Lajoie was indeed the heart of the team. For the next five years, Lajoie continued to post solid offensive statistics in Cleveland, his lowest batting average being a very respectable .289 in 1908. Still, he could not keep up with the productive bat of Ty Cobb. Cobb, who was 12 years younger than Lajoie, was turning the American League batting title into his personal possession. In 1907, Cobb's first full season with Detroit, he posted a .350 batting average. He had not yet reached his twenty-first birthday, and nearly half a century would pass before a younger man would win a major-league batting crown. To prove it was no fluke, Cobb won the batting championship again in 1908, with a relatively low .324 average. A .377 average in 1909 gave Cobb three straight titles, and there was little doubt that Cobb was no flash in the pan. By this time, Cobb had gained recognition as the American League's best player, but had also won the dubious honor of being the most hated player in the game. He was so argumentative that no one would room with him on road trips. He usually ate alone and sat by himself in the dugout. This did not mean that Cobb would not confront a fellow Tiger who he felt was not giving his best effort. Fistfights with teammates and opponents, and even a celebrated brawl with umpire Billy Evans, were all part of the Cobb psyche. As the 1910 season unfolded, it became apparent that the race for the AL batting title was a simple case of the fan favorite (Lajoie) versus the black hat (Cobb).

For both Cobb and Lajoie, the thrill of competing for the league batting title in 1910 would have to suffice. There was no way their respective clubs were going to be in pennant contention.

Connie Mack, despite short arms and deep pockets, had built a fine team in Philadelphia and was making easy work of the other seven AL clubs. The A's would finish the season in impressive fashion, winning 102 games. The second-place New York Highlanders (they were still a few years from acquiring the Yankee nickname) were well back, with 88 victories. Cobb's Tigers and Lajoie's "Naps" were mired even further back, and realized early on that the pennant belonged to Philadelphia.

Sunday, October 9, was the final day of regularly scheduled games in the American League for the 1910 season. After Saturday's game against Chicago, Ty Cobb's batting average stood at .385 (he had had 196 hits in 509 at-bats) and appeared to have the AL batting title clearly in his grasp. Nine percentage points behind was Napoleon Lajoie. His Cleveland club was to finish their schedule that Sunday with a doubleheader in St. Louis against the Browns. Not only was the honor of winning the league batting championship at stake, there was a tangible reward as well. The Chalmers Automobile Company had announced it would award one of its luxury automobiles to the AL batting king. Since these were the days in which a $5,000 salary was considered substantial by major leaguers, the car was definitely a prize worth shooting for.

Cobb, figuring his lead over Lajoie was a safe one, opted not to play in his team's final game against Chicago. A bad game might drop his average a few points and give Lajoie a more legitimate chance of catching him. (Over the years Cobb has been criticized for skipping this last game, but it has been commonly done up to the present day by batting champions who feared being overtaken at the wire.) Lajoie must have begun his day in St. Louis under the impression that Cobb's lead was insurmountable. However, on this day in St. Louis, Lajoie would discover he had a few friends in the opponents' dugout rooting for him and willing to sabotage Cobb's try for a fourth straight batting title.

Browns manager Jack O'Connor was aware that Lajoie was in need of a big day at the plate if he had any hope of challenging Cobb. In a scandalous act, he positioned a rookie named John "Red" Corriden at third base and advised him to play deep behind the bag—so deep that Corriden was actually standing in the outfield grass — whenever Lajoie came to the plate. Somehow, Lajoie failed to notice the vast uncovered area near third base the first time he batted. Nevertheless, he pounded the ball for a triple. When Lajoie returned to the bench, his teammates commented that with Corriden stationed so far back, he could bunt all afternoon and roll up lots of easy hits. The next three times up at bat, Lajoie took advantage of the Browns' generosity and recorded three bunt singles. In the first game (which St. Louis won, 5–4) Lajoie was four-for-four.

The second game of the doubleheader saw more of the same. Corriden stayed back and Lajoie continued to bunt. Two more gift hits were notched by Lajoie, who now could sense that Cobb's lead was getting tenuous. The St. Louis fans were becoming disgusted with the charity being doled out to Lajoie and the booing and jeering increased with each bunt single. The situation became absolutely farcical in Lajoie's final at-bat, when, for some reason, he decided not to bunt, but instead swung away and hit a sharp grounder to St. Louis' shortstop Bobby Wallace. Wallace did not field the ball cleanly and was charged with an error. Off the St. Louis bench charged coach Harry Howell to confront the official scorer. Howell demanded that the error be changed to a hit, but the scorer, a woman, refused to be manipulated, even though Howell offered to buy her a new wardrobe! Lajoie was credited with a hitless at-bat. His final season totals showed 227 hits in 591 at-bats for an average of .384. He had lost the batting title by the equivalent of one hit.

Needless to say, the ridiculous actions of the Browns did not go unnoticed. A St. Louis businessman offered $250 toward the purchase of a car for Cobb if the scorer's error decision happened to be changed. It wasn't. The Chalmers Automobile Company, embarrassed by the Browns' chicanery, ended up giving cars to both Cobb and Lajoie. Cobb was proclaimed the AL batting champion. It was the fourth of nine successive titles (and 12 overall) which Cobb would win in his 24 seasons in the majors. American League president Ban Johnson was not amused by the actions of Browns manager Jack O'Connor and coach Harry Howell. To them he handed down the ultimate penalty — a lifetime banishment from baseball — for trying to rig the batting championship.

Unbelievably, the members of the Browns and the Cleveland

newspaper writers tried to deny that any shenanigans had taken place. One Cleveland report in *The Cleveland Plain Dealer*, trying to justify Corriden's unusual positioning, said with all sincerity,

> In games throughout the circuit, the fielders of opposing teams have been accustomed to play far back to intercept Lajoie's terrific drives. The St. Louis third baseman was following a well-established precedent in playing [Lajoie] well back.

Corriden himself added to the farce by claiming self-defense in standing in the outfield while Lajoie was batting. He told the media,

> I want to remain in baseball for some time. I was not going to get killed playing in on Lajoie. I might have got some of Lajoie's bunts, and at the same time a broken nose or lost a couple of teeth. Lajoie is known as a hard hitter and I played far back.

Cobb remained a dominant force in the sport until his retirement in 1928. He retained the anger and fury which drove him to be baseball's most consistent hitter. If he ever needed any additional motivation to succeed, the blatant attempt by the St. Louis Browns to rob him of a batting crown in 1910 certainly provided it.

In a strange postscript to the story, the controversy reemerged in 1981. Seventy-one years after the dubious shenanigans of the St. Louis Browns had apparently failed to deprive Cobb of the 1910 AL batting title, researchers for *The Sporting News* discovered that Lajoie actually did finish ahead of Cobb in the batting race! By going meticulously through the official American League boxscores for each of Detroit's and Cleveland's games in 1910, they discovered that one game, in which Cobb had managed to get two hits, had accidentally been counted twice! When Cobb's batting average was recalculated, it stood at .383, one point below Lajoie's.

Despite this conclusive mathematical evidence that Lajoie truly finished ahead of Cobb in the 1910 AL batting race, a special commissioner's committee unanimously decided not to alter history. Presumably, the committee did not want to reward the long-dead

Lajoie for the assistance the St. Louis Browns had given him on the last day of the season. Cobb, who died in 1961, was still listed as winning the 1910 AL batting championship, with Lajoie a close second.

Further research on Cobb's career uncovered the fact that he had been shortchanged out of a hit during his rookie season in 1905. This oversight, combined with the important 1910 miscalculation, now places Cobb's career hit total at 4,190 instead of the 4,191 he had always been credited as having. Pete Rose's much-publicized 4,192nd hit off San Diego's Eric Show in 1985, which put him ahead of Cobb, was actually gravy. Rose's 4,191st hit, delivered by Chicago's Reggie Patterson a few days earlier, had put him over the top.

Chapter 5

The Lifetime Banishment of Buck Weaver and Joe Jackson (1919 World Series)

Innocent but Still Guilty:

> Regardless of the verdict of juries, no player that undertakes or promises to throw a ball game; no player that sits in a conference with a bunch of crooked players and gamblers where the ways and means of throwing games are planned and discussed and does not promptly tell his club about it, will ever play professional baseball.
>
> —From commissioner Kenesaw Landis' edict which barred the eight "Black Sox" from organized baseball for life. Quoted in *Eight Men Out*.

The most shameful incident in the history of major-league baseball occurred in October of 1919, when a number of players on the American League champion Chicago White Sox conspired with gamblers to deliberately lose the World Series to the National League champion Cincinnati Reds. When details of the underhanded scheme became known and an investigation was launched, eight Chicago players (known to the public as the Black Sox) were handed the ultimate penalty by the sport's first commissioner—permanent banishment from the sport. There is overwhelming evidence that six of the Black Sox did indeed plan and participate in the most notorious scandal ever to rock American sports, but there is precious little evidence that "Shoeless" Joe Jackson or George "Buck" Weaver deliberately played to lose in the autumn of 1919. Nevertheless, both Jackson and Weaver received the same harsh punishment as the other six players, and had glorious careers snuffed out forever.

The story of the 1919 World Series resurfaced during the 1980s when two popular baseball movies, *Eight Men Out* and *Field of Dreams*, rehashed some of the details of the scandal. To casual fans of the game, Shoeless Joe Jackson was just a name from the dim past. Best known to moviegoers as the ballplayer who emerged from the Iowa corn field to have a chat with Kevin Costner in *Field of Dreams*, his true-life exploits are buried in the murky past. "Shoeless Joe Jackson? He was one of the crooks in the 1919 World Series," an uninformed fan might say. But that fan could probably not elaborate on Jackson's career.

The record books say that Joseph Jefferson Jackson was born in Pickens County, South Carolina, on July 16, 1889. The accuracy of the date is open to speculation. The years 1887 and 1888 have also appeared in biographies of Shoeless Joe, and could be correct just as easily as the 1889 date. Working in textile mills instead of attending school, Jackson never learned how to read or write. He did excel, however, in playing baseball for local clubs, whose managers were quick to notice that the teenage Jackson could hit a ball harder, farther, and more consistently than the grown men he played with and against. Professional baseball was the obvious next step for young Joe. After he humiliated one pitcher after another as a member of the New Orleans club in the Southern League, his contract was picked up by Connie Mack, the owner-manager of the Philadelphia Athletics. Jackson played in five games at the end of the 1908 season and prepared to become a regular member of the A's outfield in 1909. However, the cruel taunts of his teammates regarding his illiteracy and impoverished upbringing affected Jackson's self-esteem deeply. He left Philadelphia after just five games of the 1909 season, his career apparently over.

Granted his release from the Athletics in 1910, Jackson joined Cleveland in time to play in 20 games. Because of the relatively few major league games Jackson had played in the three previous seasons, he was still considered a rookie in 1911. And what a rookie season he had! Jackson batted .408 and rapped out 233 hits, displaying the talents that Connie Mack had seen and that the residents of rural South Carolina knew he possessed. To prove 1911 had been no fluke, Jackson had another fabulous season in 1912, batting .395 and stroking 226 hits. Combining his technically flawless left-handed swing with God-given speed, Jackson led the AL in triples that season, with 26. He continued to post impressive numbers for Cleveland through the middle of 1915, when he was unexpectedly traded to the Chicago White Sox for three mediocre players and $31,000. The change of scenery did not affect Jackson's production in the slightest. With the exception of 1917, when his batting average dipped to .301, Jackson wielded a hot bat in Chicago, usually batting well over .340. When he wasn't demoralizing opponents with his bat, his speed did the trick. Never mind the 202 stolen bases in his shortened career; Jackson's speed was best used in the outfield, where balls that had double or triple written all over them somehow found their way into Jackson's glove with regularity. Some writers were saying that Jackson was a better all-around player than either Ty Cobb or Nap Lajoie.

Buck Weaver did not have to endure the rough start in the big leagues which had hurt Jackson. Arriving in Chicago in 1912, Weaver immediately became the club's regular shortstop, although his rookie season saw him commit 71 errors. The error total declined slightly over the next three seasons, eventually to 49 in 1915. In 1916, Weaver split the season between shortstop and third base, which improved his fielding percentage considerably. By 1919, Weaver, now the club's regular third baseman, was part of a solid White Sox infield. He had made only 20 errors, a good figure considering how primitive fielders' gloves were at that time. He had also become a decent contact hitter, usually batting in the .270 range. With star players such as catcher Ray Schalk, second baseman Eddie Collins, and talented pitchers Eddie Cicotte and Lefty Williams, the White Sox were clear betting favorites to defeat Cincinnati in the 1919 World Series, at least in the early wagering. Then the odds began to slowly but dramatically shift in favor of the Reds. Why?

The odds began to shift for two reasons. First, the gamblers orchestrating the fix were wagering heavily on Cincinnati. Second, rumors of the fix were widely circulating. Gamblers who were not involved in the conspiracy, and who would have bet on Chicago, were either scared off by the rumors and made no bets, or followed the prevailing trend and put money on the Reds.

Several notable figures initiated the fix, each one later telling a slightly different story than the others. It is clear that one-time pitcher "Sleepy" Bill Burns and former boxers Billy Maharg and Abe Attell were aware that numerous White Sox players were disgusted with penny-pinching owner Charles Comiskey. Despite having the AL's most talented club and winning the 1917 World Series, Comiskey paid his players poorly. Star players for other clubs were making between $5,000 and $6,000 per season. Some of Comiskey's best players took home just $2,400. Comiskey even undercut his players when it came to meal money on road trips. Among the most disenchanted players was pitcher Eddie Cicotte, the winner of 29 games for the White Sox in 1919. Promised a large bonus if he won 30 games in 1919, Comiskey ordered manager Kid Gleason to bench Cicotte as soon as he reached the 29-win plateau to ensure that the thirtieth victory would never come.

First baseman Chick Gandil and shortstop Swede Risberg were approached by Burns and Maharg, who claimed they could pay $5,000 to each player on the White Sox who agreed to "take it easy" in the upcoming World Series. Apparently, Gandil persuaded Cicotte to go along with the scheme. Outfielder Happy Felsch agreed to the fix as well. Lefty Williams, told by Gandil and Risberg that the World Series was as good as lost with Cicotte and the others purposely trying to lose, was also accepted into the conspiracy. Utility infielder Fred McMullin accidentally overheard the conspirators and demanded to be let in on the deal as well. Buck Weaver was invited to dump the series too, but adamantly refused. Financially backed by Boston gambler "Sport" Sullivan and New York's Arnold Rothstein, Burns and Attell agreed to pay the conspirators in full before Game One. Gandil had informed Burns that he could also cajole Joe Jackson into intentionally losing, which would absolutely guarantee Cincinnati the 1919 World Series.

Jackson, so the story goes, was informed by Gandil that the fix was in and he might as well get his share of the profits. Jackson, ignorant of the policies of major-league clubs, did not quite know what to do about it. Instead of reporting the conspiracy to Comiskey, Jackson dressed for Game One and, shortly before the game, told manager Kid Gleason he did not wish to play. Gleason, stunned, ordered Jackson to take the field. With Cicotte pitching batting-practice fastballs, Cincinnati won the opener of the best-of-nine series by a 9–1 score. Lefty Williams walked three Reds in the decisive fourth inning of Game Two to allow Cincinnati to win, 4–2. The gamblers who were wise to the fix were delighted, but the White Sox weren't. Having received only a fraction of their promised bribe money, the Sox conspirators rebelled in Game Three and won, 3–0, as Dickie Kerr hurled the shutout.

When more money trickled in for the crooked players for Games Four and Five, Cicotte and Williams kept their promises to perform poorly. Cicotte lost Game Four, 2–0, and Williams lost Game Five, 5–0. When no more bribe money was forthcoming, Chicago won Game Six, 5–4, and Cicotte won Game Seven, 4–1. The gamblers, alarmed that their long-term bets were in jeopardy, are said to have threatened Lefty Williams, Chicago's scheduled starter in Game Eight, and his family with physical harm if he did not lose the next game. Thoroughly intimidated, Williams cooperated, allowing four runs in the first inning while retiring only one batter before being relieved. Cincinnati rolled to an easy 10–5 victory to take the 1919 World Series five games to three.

The season was over and nothing much was said about the events of October 1919, until September of 1920, when reporters, skeptical of the White Sox' poor play, launched an investigation and those involved started to talk. Probably the most talkative was Bill Burns, who had lost a fortune betting on Cincinnati in Game Three, the afternoon when the fixers rebelled because their payoff had not arrived. The guilty players, with no legal counsel, were persuaded that their careers could be salvaged if they signed written confessions. Among those who signed was Joe Jackson, even though he had not agreed to actively fix any games and, according to his biographer, Donald Gropman, had tried to turn in his bribe money to owner Comiskey. A grand jury was convened to hear the case. Somehow, the players' confessions were "lost" and a verdict of not guilty came down on the eight White Sox. (There were eight because Buck Weaver, although not participating in the fix, had knowledge of it and did not report it to Comiskey.) The players rejoiced. Their careers were salvaged! Baseball could continue for them as it always had!

Not so fast, said Judge Kenesaw Mountain Landis. In order to restore the sport's good name, the owners had agreed to turn over much of their power to the flamboyant judge, and appointed him Commissioner of Baseball for life. Just as the eight "Black Sox" were looking forward to the 1921 season, Landis made his famous pronouncement: "Regardless of the verdict of juries," the eight players had willfully involved themselves with gamblers, or players connected with gamblers, and were forever barred from professional baseball.

While the owners applauded this drastic decree, others were horrified. *Regardless of the verdict of juries?* Didn't that contradict everything that American justice supposedly stood for? Appeal after appeal was launched on behalf of the players, but the sentence stood. None of the eight players ever appeared in another major-league game, although it is generally accepted that some, including Jackson, got into a few minor-league games under false names.

Fans of Shoeless Joe Jackson were devastated. Just in his early thirties, he had at least several good years ahead of him. In his final season, 1920, Jackson had batted .382. His overall career average was .356, the third highest of all time. Did Jackson play below his best during the eight-game 1919 World Series? Look at the statistics and decide for yourself. In 32 at-bats, Jackson recorded 12 hits, for a more-than-respectable .375 batting average. He also hit three doubles and the only home run of the 1919 World Series. Only twice did Jackson strike out. Defensively, Jackson had 16 putouts and one assist. He made *no errors*. Fellow outfielder Happy Felsch, an active participant in the fix, made two errors.

What about Buck Weaver? There was certainly no indication that he was trying to lose. He handled 27 chances (nine putouts and 18 assists) in the series and committed no errors. Weaver's batting average was almost as good as Jackson's. At the plate, Weaver had 11 hits in 34 at-bats (including four doubles and a triple) for a batting average of .324, well above his career average of .272. Nevertheless, both Jackson and Weaver were deemed to be undesirable to organized baseball at any level. When word leaked to Commissioner Landis that Jackson was being employed as a batting coach by a Class D club—the lowest level of pro baseball—Landis immediately ordered the team to fire Jackson. Even petitions from congressmen from Jackson's home state of South Carolina, asking Landis to at least reexamine Jackson's case, fell on deaf ears. Jackson died in 1951, still trying to have his name cleared. To date, some four decades after his death, Jackson is still on baseball's ineligible list.

So is Buck Weaver. When the 1920 season ended, Weaver was just 30 years old and, like Jackson, probably could have been a productive player for several more seasons. Until his death in 1956, Weaver, along with members of his family and sympathetic fans, tried to have his status changed from ineligible to eligible. Like Jackson, he, too, had no success, and his name is still linked with Swede Risberg's and Chick Gandil's, even though he never received a penny for participating in the fix and was never even a part of it.

"I'd give a million dollars to undo the things I've done," said Eddie Cicotte late in life, as quoted in *Baseball Digest*. He had been guilty, but he was remorseful. Inspired by the niggardly ways of owner Comiskey, he had been talked into forfeiting his baseball future by Gandil in return for precious little. In the cases of Joe Jackson and Buck Weaver, the result was much worse. They played the 1919 World Series to win. They played it well, too. Yet circumstances and Judge Landis' harsh ruling derailed their careers. Jackson would certainly have ended up in Cooperstown with Ruth, Cobb, Lajoie, Speaker, Sisler, and the other greats who played in his era. Sadly, Jackson is now known to most casual fans because of Hollywood. The irony is that his career, just like the career of Buck Weaver, did not have a Hollywood ending.

Chapter 6

Darkness at the Polo Grounds: George Hildebrand Calls the Game (1922 World Series)

> The umpire-in-chief [plate umpire] shall be the sole judge as to whether and when play shall be suspended during a game because of unsuitable weather conditions or the unfit condition of the playing field.
>
> —*The Official Rules of Baseball*, Rule 3.10 (c)

If one takes the time and trouble to read through baseball's complex rule book, one particular phrase will become very familiar to the reader. That phrase is "in the opinion of the umpire." Those who authored those august rules and have altered them over the years were wise in including this phrase so often. It makes it clear that decisions on the playing field are not arrived at through the democratic process. The umpiring crew, in theory, is a mini-dictatorship whose powers control the game and run it in an orderly fashion. A ball game truly could not run smoothly if the umpires did not have their dictatorial powers. Players learn at an early age that what the umpire says is law, especially regarding judgment calls. And, of course, judgment calls comprise much of what takes place in a game, from the top of the first inning until the bottom of the ninth.

Over the years, the system has worked rather well at all levels. Disputes regarding safes and outs do occur, but the decision ultimately rests with the official who made the call, and most of the time managers who attempt to argue these calls realize that their chances of having such a call overturned are negligible. The rule book also bestows special powers on the man it refers to as the "umpire-in-chief," whom we know as the plate umpire. Under these extraordinary provisions, the plate umpire, and he alone, has the authority to forfeit games (fortunately, this is rarely invoked) and the power to suspend or halt games because of poor weather, bad or dangerous field conditions, and darkness. To many modern fans of baseball, the idea of a major league game being stopped on account of darkness is something beyond their experience. When the Chicago Cubs finally installed lights at venerable Wrigley Field in the late 1980s, the last vestiges of daytime-only games disappeared from the majors. Up until 1935, when the Cincinnati Reds hosted the Philadelphia Phillies in the majors' first night game, darkness presented real problems to umpiring crews, especially in late-season games, when the hours of daylight became increasingly shorter. It was a harsh reality that some games had to be stopped before their natural conclusion simply because the ball could no longer be seen by players, umpires, and spectators.

Rule 3.10 (c) makes it perfectly clear that the decision regarding when a game should be stopped is not an exact science. It is one of those numerous decisions that lie within the umpire's discretion, specifically, the plate umpire's. Before the introduction of night baseball, major-league umpires were more than familiar with having to make delicate decisions on this matter. Should the game be halted here? Can we squeeze another full inning in before the park becomes completely dark? Naturally, disputes would arise over such decisions. One manager would insist that there was still plenty of daylight to continue the game (naturally, his club would be the one on the short end of the score), while his counterpart in the other dugout would declare that he could no longer read his lineup cards. Thus it was left up to the wisdom of the umpire-in-chief to settle the matter and opt to either terminate the game or continue it as darkness began to envelop the playing field.

The World Series, as we know it, made its debut in 1903, long before anybody ever dreamed of playing major-league baseball under artificial floodlights. Traditionalists dominated the major-league hierarchy through the mid-century, and it wasn't until 1971 that the World Series' first night game was played. Lights had been available in most big-league parks by the 1940s and had, on occasion, to be turned on during World Series play to ensure that games could be continued. The coming of lights had, for all intents and purposes, eliminated the need for Rule 3.10 (c) in World Series games by the mid–1940s. However, this luxury did not exist in the early days of the World Series. Darkness was as much a threat to a long game in the series as it was during the regular season. On three different occasions—once in 1907, once in 1912, and once in 1922—World Series games were terminated because of darkness. In all three cases, the games were tied at the point of stoppage, thus not giving a cheap win to either team. That does not mean, however, that there was no controversy following the decisions. The 1922 "darkness" call by umpire George Hildebrand so outraged spectators and the commissioner's office that umpiring crews felt themselves under the gun in every World Series game played in an unlighted park from that day forward. No man in blue wanted to be another George Hildebrand.

The 1922 World Series should have been one of baseball's finest showcases up to that time. Its two most glamorous teams, John McGraw's talented New York Giants, the pride of Manhattan, and the New York Yankees, the new darlings of the American League, were pitted against each other. For both clubs, 1922 would mark their second straight appearance in the World Series. The previous October, the favored Giants had managed to defeat the young Yankees five games to three in a best-of-nine affair (the 1921 World Series was the last season in which five victories were required to win the title). The very fact that the Yankees, once the poor relation to New York's Giants, were even competitive was a disturbing sign to McGraw. His clubs had dominated the baseball scene in New York for two full decades, and he resented the idea that they might have to share the sports-page glory with their American League neighbors.

McGraw's club looked as menacing as ever going into the 1922 World Series. Determined to defend their championship, the Giants had put together a solid season, finishing seven full games in front of the Cincinnati Reds. There was hardly a weakness among the Giant regulars that year. Even though no Giant finished in the top five among National League batting-average leaders, seven of the eight regulars had averages above .300. The lone exception was third baseman Heinie Groh, who batted a respectable .265. McGraw could also count on his reliable pitching staff. Art Nehf won 19 games, Rosie Ryan won 17, Jesse Barnes won 13, and Shufflin' Phil Douglas (the National League's leader in earned run average) finished off his career with 11 wins. Irish Meusel's clutch hitting won a fair share of the Giants' 93 victories in 1922. Meusel finished in the top five in the league in triples, home runs, and total bases. Meusel's teammate Dave Bancroft was no slouch either, ranking among the NL's best in hits, doubles, and runs scored.

Nevertheless, the Giants would be tested by the Yankees and their diminutive manager, Miller Huggins. Although the Yankees were a far cry from the powerful machine they would be in a few short years, they had enough talent in 1922 to win 94 games and squeak out a pennant win over the St. Louis Browns by one thin game. The Yankees relied on superior pitching to lift them to their second straight AL flag. Bullet Joe Bush notched 26 victories, the second-best total in the league. Twenty more games were won by Bob Shawkey. Not far behind was 19-game winner Waite Hoyt. Despite the talent on the mound for the 1922 Yankees, it was an ex-pitcher who received most of the publicity. Babe Ruth had become the focal point of everything the Yankees did. As a skinny member of the Boston Red Sox in 1919, the Babe had shocked the baseball community by hitting 29 home runs, an unheard-of total at the time. Upon being sold to the Yankees by cash-strapped Red Sox owner Harry Frazee in 1920, Ruth opened up the golden age of sports by blasting 54 home runs. In 1921, Ruth upped the ante to 59 homers, and was singlehandedly altering the face of the game. For years, baseball had been a game of moving each runner a base at a time. Now Ruth had come along and ably demonstrated how efficient a soaring drive toward the outfield bleachers could be.

Ruth, in 1922, was 27 years old and probably at his athletic peak. However, his waistline was expanding as fast as his reputation, and 1922 was an off year for the Babe—by his lofty standards, anyway. He had managed "only" 35 home runs and 99 runs batted in. Ruth's declining fitness combined with an early-season suspension by the all-powerful baseball commissioner, Judge Kenesaw Mountain Landis, for participating in an illegal barnstorming tour, was responsible for the notable decline in the Babe's offensive totals. Still, Ruth would have to be held in check if the Giants were to repeat as World Series champions, and McGraw knew it.

Since both the Yankees and the Giants shared the same home park, the entire 1922 World Series would be contested at the Polo Grounds. The Giants were the "home team" for Game One, on October 4, and were hard pressed to win it by a 3–2 margin. Trailing 2–0 in the bottom of the eighth, the Giants rallied for three runs. Two of them were driven in by an Irish Meusel single, and the decisive run came on a timely sacrifice fly by Ross Youngs. Rosie Ryan relieved Giants starter Art Nehf for the victory.

New York City was buzzing with baseball excitement. Its two major league clubs were battling it out in a "subway series" to determine bragging rights, not only for the city but for the major-league baseball world. Game Two attracted a huge throng of forty thousand to the Polo Grounds and a record gate of $120,000 poured through the cashiers' wickets. In the end, neither the Giants nor the Yankees, nor the businessmen who operated big-league baseball, would see a penny of that sum.

Game Two lived up to the excitement of Game One. The Giants roared off to a big 3–0 lead in the top of the first inning, Irish Meusel's three-run homer accounting for the damage. The Yankees pushed a run across in the bottom half of the first, to narrow the Giants' lead to 3–1. A solo home run by Yankee second baseman Aaron Ward in the fourth inning made it 3–2. Spectacular fielding by both teams stifled rally after rally until the Yankees scored a third run in the bottom of the eighth to tie the score. Both teams failed to tally in the ninth, sending the game into extra innings. At 4:45 P.M., the tenth inning concluded with the score still tied at 3–3. The sun was still high in the sky and at least 45 minutes of daylight remained. This did not seem to enter into plate umpire George Hildebrand's reasoning, though, as he picked up the ball following the late out in the tenth, and declared the game over because of "darkness," after two hours and 41 minutes.

The spectators were as amazed as the players. Then anger set in. An Associated Press account best summed up the mood of the crowd when they realized the thrilling game they were enjoying would end without a winner.

> After the game, thousands of fans gathered in front of the press box and the stands and gave a demonstration against the action of the officials in calling the game. Thousands gathered in front of Commissioner Landis' box and jeered him continuously for several minutes. It was a scene unparalleled in World Series history. The fans claim that it was a pure move to get another 40,000 into the park for an extra game, and that at least two more innings could have been played.

Commissioner Landis was the most visible target of the unruly and disenchanted spectators. To them, Landis represented the sport's ultimate power. If anyone could overturn such a discretionary decision by the umpires, it was he. Landis, despite being baseball's czar, knew his office could do nothing to overturn a judgment call on the field. So he simply sat in his box, as angry as any of the forty thousand paying patrons at the Polo Grounds, and accepted the crowd's insults. The newspaper account continued,

> Landis was visibly uncomfortable, but he would not answer the questions hurled at him by the fans wanting to know what he was going to do about it. The mob increased in front of the Commissioner's box and defied the special police who tried to get them to leave the field....
>
> Landis, with two or three special policemen fighting to keep back the crowd, was jostled and buffeted by angry men. He stopped several times and faced the mob, shouting back at them and flourishing his cane over his head.

Once Landis got safely away from the crowd, he confronted umpire Hildebrand, demanding to know why he had decided to stop the game. According to Hildebrand and quoted in *Baseball Anecdotes*, "a haze had descended over the field" which had impelled him to halt the contest. There was nothing Landis could do to overturn Hildebrand's verdict, but he privately told the three umpires (Hildebrand, Bill Klem, and William McCormick) that he wanted no further interruptions of games in the World Series. In order to pacify those who believed Hildebrand's decision was designed to add another game to the Series and generate more money for the players and owners, Landis made the extraordinary gesture of donating the entire gate receipts from Game Two of the World Series to various war charities in New York City.

The Giants won Game Three 3–0, to take a 2–0 lead in games. In Game Four, the umpires had a problem. "Saturday's game . . . should not have been played," opened an Associated Press report. "Rain fell throughout the contest, and at times almost amounted to a downpour." Heeding Landis' advice, the umpires had ordered that the game be played despite the mud. The Giants won Game Four 4–3, and the next day won 5–3, to complete an odd four-game sweep of the Yankees, one which took five games. Ruth was held to just two hits in 17 at-bats, and the Giants were once again the toast of New York City. Of more lasting importance, though, is the fact that no postseason game was ever stopped due to darkness after that "hazy" afternoon in the Polo Grounds in 1922, when George Hildebrand's decision cost the sport a fortune, and almost cost it its integrity.

Chapter 7

Sam Rice's Vanishing Act: Was It a Catch or a Home Run? (1925 World Series)

Take a strong wind, a critical World Series game, a sharply hit baseball, a disappearing outfielder, and testimony from beyond the grave, and what do you have? Well, you either have the plot for a bad movie or you have the key ingredients of one of baseball's hottest and most enduring controversies. It has been nearly 70 years since Sam Rice, a talented outfielder who was a key member of Washington's back-to-back pennant-winning teams, made (or did not make) the most controversial catch in the history of the World Series—arguably the most controversial catch in the long history of major league baseball.

The 1925 World Series was a refreshing change for many baseball fans. For the first time since the scandalous 1919 series, the Fall Classic would be contested without a New York–based club. The New York Giants, under the managerial genius of John McGraw, had dominated the National League since 1921, capturing every NL title from 1921 to 1924. During that period, the American League pennant seemed to be the sole property of the other New York club, the upstart Yankees, who has risen from nowhere to win three straight AL flags, from 1921 to 1923. The long-ball hitting exploits of George Herman "Babe" Ruth, acquired from the Boston Red Sox in 1920, had a lot to do with the dramatic turnaround of the team, which would soon be known informally as the Bronx Bombers. The dominance of the New York franchises began to wane in 1924, at least in part, when the American League's perennial doormats, the Washington Senators, finally won a pennant for aging fireball pitcher Walter Johnson. In a series which featured many twists of fate, Johnson's Senators managed to squeak out a narrow seven-game victory over McGraw's Giants. In typical storybook fashion, Walter Johnson won the finale in a rare relief stint in extra innings.

So when the Senators repeated their pennant-winning form in 1925, they were considered the seasoned veterans. The upstarts from Pittsburgh—Pie Traynor, Kiki Cuyler and company, who had managed to end the Giants' four-year grip on the National League pennant—were thought to be the underdogs as the 1925 World Series opened in Pittsburgh's Forbes Field. Sentimental favorite Walter Johnson disappointed the hometown Pirates fans, but pleased those who now considered him a legend, by hurling a complete-game 4–1 victory for the Senators in Game One. In Game Two, Pittsburgh's Vic Aldridge and Washington's Stan Coveleski both threw complete games, but Aldridge's club outscored the Senators 3–2 to even the series at one game apiece. Game Three would shift to Griffith Stadium in Washington. There Sam Rice would be the key figure in one of baseball's most controversial episodes.

Saturday, October 10, 1925, was a particularly miserable day in Washington, D.C. Idealists who visualize World Series games being played in lovely autumn sunshine would have been disappointed. The weather at Griffith Stadium was unusually cold, but this was only part of the story. A severe wind was blasting out toward right field, adding to the discomfort of players, spectators, and the mixed crew of National and American League umpires, who would soon have the unenviable task of having to rule on a play that none of them had adequately seen.

Pittsburgh pushed a run across the plate in the second inning to open the scoring. Washington evened the score in the third. By the top of the sixth inning, two notable events had occurred: the high winds had ripped a section off the grandstand's roof, and the Pirates had taken a 3–1 lead. Washington managed to fight back with a single run in the bottom of the sixth, and added two more in the seventh to assume a tenuous 4–3 lead. Alex Ferguson, who had pitched the first seven innings for the Senators, left the game in the top of the eighth in favor of reliever Firpo Marberry. Washington also made a relatively minor defensive change—but one that would pay huge dividends. Starting center fielder Sam Rice was shifted to right field and Earl McNeely replaced Rice in center field.

With one out in the top of the eighth inning, the Pittsburgh catcher, Earl Smith, entered the batter's box to face Marberry. Smith had batted a respectable .313 during the regular season and had managed to hit eight home runs. Smith probably figured he had hit his first World Series home run when he connected solidly with one of Marberry's pitches and sent a long, deep drive to right-center field. With the gusting wind adding to the length of the hit, it seemed certain that the ball would land in the bleacher seats for a game-tying homer. However, Rice got a good jump on the ball and was in full flight, chasing it toward the low outfield wall which separated the playing field in Griffith Stadium from the cheap seats. Rice's glove connected with the ball just as his body collided with the barrier. The momentum of the crash propelled Rice into the stands, where he disappeared from the sight of most of the spectators and all of the umpiring crew.

For an extended period of time—some writers claim it was as long as 30 seconds—Sam Rice was gone from the field of play. He was not totally invisible, however. His legs were, rather comically, sticking straight up in the air, while his torso was resting on or near the first row of bleacher seats. The burning question that now pervaded all corners of Griffith Stadium was not whether Rice was injured (he was not), but whether he had caught the ball to deprive Earl Smith of a crucial home run.

Veteran National League umpire Charlie Rigler ran from his position at second base all the way out to the right-center field wall to determine whether or not Rice had made a legitimate catch. (It is important to remember that umpire Rigler was a National League umpire and that Rice was an American League player.) Rigler was approaching the outfield wall when Rice appeared back on the field, under his own power, with the ball in his glove. Without any hesitation, Rigler declared Smith out. Washington still led 4–3.

Needless to say, the Pirates did not accept umpire Rigler's decision quietly. The game was delayed for a full 15 minutes—an exceptionally prolonged argument—while Rigler tried to explain his decision to one angry Pirate after another. Pittsburgh manager Bill McKechnie, having had no luck in persuading Rigler to change his verdict, attempted to convince the remainder of the umpiring crew to overrule the call. No umpire, of course, has the power or authority to change the call of a fellow umpire—especially on a judgment call. Furthermore, there was absolutely no clear evidence on which to change the call from "out" to "home run."

In making the "out" call, Rigler was simply adhering to an old umpiring adage: if you are prevented from seeing whether a ball is caught or not, and the player presents the ball either in his glove or bare hand, assume it was a legal catch. Rigler, when he saw Rice emerge from the bleachers, noted that the ball was in Rice's glove. Under the circumstances, Rigler had no choice but to make the "out" call. If an umpire had been swift enough to get to the wall when Rice and the ball did (a physical impossibility), the umpire would have had to determine whether Rice had maintained control of the ball before he crashed into the seats. By rule, if Rice had lost control of the ball, even for a moment, after he had fallen over the barrier, the catch would have been nullified and the play declared a home run. Rigler, probably to his great relief, could not possibly see whether Rice had bobbled the ball in the stands, and based his "out" call solely on the fact that Rice reappeared in the outfield with the ball in his glove.

After 15 minutes of utterly futile protests by the Pirates, the game resumed. There was no further scoring. Washington won 4–3, to take a 2–1 lead in the 1925 World Series. However, the controversy did not die.

Rice's catch was clearly the main story of the game, and for eager newspaper reporters it was a chance to attempt to seek the truth about a very mysterious situation. The press corps was about evenly divided. Half thought Rice's catch was legitimate, the other half was doubtful. To the handful of Pittsburgh fans who happened to be seated in the outfield bleachers, the situation was clear, in their minds at least: Sam Rice had fooled umpire Rigler. Several fans offered written testimony that Rice had not maintained possession of the ball after falling into the seats. Affidavits were sent to Baseball Commissioner Kenesaw Mountain Landis in hope that the man who had cleaned up the 1919 Black Sox Scandal would rule in favor of the Pirates. But even the most powerful man in organized baseball had no authority to change an umpire's judgment call. Sam Rice's catch stood, and so did Washington's 4–3 victory.

In some ways, the rest of the 1925 World Series worked toward diffusing the controversial catch. In Game Four, Walter Johnson pitched a shutout for a 4–0 Senators win, giving Washington a seemingly insurmountable lead of three games to one. Nevetheless, Pittsburgh rebounded to win the remaining three games by scores of 6–3, 3–2, and 9–7. In all three games Washington held the lead, only to witness the pesky Pirates stage comebacks. The loss in Game Seven must have been especially galling to the Senators. They led 4–0 after the top of the first inning and 6–3 going into the bottom of the fifth, only to watch their hopes of a second straight World Series title fade away.

The question remained, however. Did Rice really make a legitimate catch in Game Three? Rice, a man who preferred to stay out of the spotlight, was always agonizingly evasive on this issue. Long after his playing days were over, friends, teammates, total strangers, and even Commissioner Landis tried to pry the truth out of him. Rice was quoted in *The World Series* as saying, "The umpire said I caught the ball."

Sam Rice had a very successful career—a Hall of Fame career, in fact. His solid leadership and nearly 3,000 career hits earned him a coveted spot among the greats enshrined in Cooperstown. But there was really only one topic that baseball fans wished to discuss with Sam Rice: the catch. Apparently tired of the whole controversy, Rice came up with an ingenious way of settling the matter once and for all, while still maintaining his love for privacy. In 1965—40 years after that cold and windy day at Griffith Stadium—Rice penned a letter to Paul Kerr, the curator of the National Baseball Hall of Fame in Cooperstown, New York. Rice sealed the letter and wrote on it, "To be opened after my death." To fans old enough to remember the controversy, there was no doubt that Rice was going to finally tell the truth about Earl Smith's fly ball—and he would do it from the grave!

Nine years went by. On October 13, 1974, Sam Rice, the Hall of Fame outfielder of the now-defunct Washington Senators, died in Rossmor, Maryland, at the ripe old age of 84. His major league career had spanned 20 seasons and he had been a member of three pennant winning teams in Washington. Yet his historical significance was largely resting on a simple letter he had written nine years before about something that had occurred in the space of a few seconds during the Calvin Coolidge administration! Rice's letter was opened. It was printed in *The World Series* and said, in part:

> The ball was a line drive headed for the bleachers toward right center. . . . I jumped as high as I could and backhanded . . . but my feet hit the barrier. . . . *At no time did I lose possession of the ball.*

There it was! Rice, according to Rice, had caught Earl Smith's line drive. The controversy was finally settled after nearly 50 years. Or was it? If Rice had indeed caught the ball, why didn't he loudly proclaim this from the first day? Why all the mystery and enigmatic answers? Who knows? And yet, why should we doubt Sam Rice's story? He said he caught Smith's line drive, and so did umpire Charlie Rigler. Shouldn't that be enough? What about the legion of Pittsburgh supporters who adamantly insisted that Rice did not catch Smith's drive? Perhaps their motive—sheer homerism—should be questioned as much as Rice's honesty.

Nevertheless, there is probably some Pittsburgh fan—a very old Pittsburgh fan—who is sitting at home right now telling a grandchild or great-grandchild, "You know, I was right there in the bleachers at old Griffith Stadium during the '25 Series, and I can tell you for a fact that Sam Rice didn't catch that ball!"

Chapter 8

The "Quick Pitch" Controversy: Did Babe Ruth Receive Preferential Treatment? (1928 World Series)

> A quick return pitch is one made with the obvious attempt to catch a batter off balance. It is an illegal pitch.
>
> —*The Official Rules of Baseball*, Rule 2.00

> Umpires will judge a quick pitch as one delivered before the batter is reasonably set in the batter's box. The quick pitch is dangerous and should not be permitted.
>
> —*The Official Rules of Baseball*, Rule 8.05 (e)

Keen observers of all team sports, not just baseball, tend to become aware of the fact that the rule book does not necessarily apply equally to all athletes at all times. Popular opinion states that the sport's premier players—superstars, if you like—often have the rules bent or stretched to accommodate their special talents. In short, there is a common belief that a hidden set of rules is applied to the stars of the game which do not apply to the average players. Don't the star quarterbacks in the National Football League seem to get away with intentional grounding while the third-stringers get flagged for the same play? Didn't Michael Jordan violate the rule against traveling on occasion without being penalized? Isn't it odd that a defenseman in the National Hockey League can level an opposing forward with a crunching body check without gaining the referee's attention?—except, of course, if he happens to make the check on Mario Lemieux or Wayne Gretzky, then off to the penalty box he goes.

Baseball players know that this phenomenon is a reality in their sport, too. The strike zone seems to expand if Greg Maddux, Roger Clemens, or Dennis Eckersley is on the mound. The same strike zone tends shrink dramatically, oddly enough, if Wade Boggs, Don Mattingly, or Tony Gwynn is the fellow standing within the lines of the batter's box. This tendency to favor the game's elite is nothing new. Joe DiMaggio was said to get his share of favorable calls from homeplate umpires who were in awe of his reputation. The pitch had to be a ball, they reasoned, if the impeccable eye of the great DiMaggio told him not to swing at it. Cobb, Hornsby, Sisler, and Speaker also probably got the benefit of the doubt on close pitches. It is not fair, of course, but it is part of the game, and a part that will likely persevere as long as baseball does.

Realizing that star treatment is somewhat enshrined within the game, one must ask oneself where the line between bending the rules for star players and making a mockery of the game is drawn. If the question had been put to the members of the 1928 St. Louis Cardinals after that season's World Series against the power-laden New York Yankees, it is quite likely that many of them would have thought that the line had been blurred in one particular at-bat for Babe Ruth, a single plate appearance that may have ensured the Yankees' winning of the world championship that year.

The 1928 American League season must have been a thoroughly frustrating one for Connie Mack's Philadelphia Athletics and Dan Howley's St. Louis Browns. Both the A's and the Brownies had very respectable teams who performed admirably throughout the long, hot summer. The Athletics were building the foundation of a solid club, one that would capture three consecutive AL flags beginning in 1929. The Browns had one of the few successful campaigns in their dreary history, winning 82 of their 154 games and finishing a solid third in the pennant chase. The A's did even better, compiling a stellar record of 98 wins and 55 losses, figures which ordinarily would win a league title comfortably. Unfortunately for Connie Mack's players, 98 wins gave them only the runner-up prize. Despite the outstanding season turned in by the Athletics in 1928, the New York Yankees captured their second consecutive AL championship by winning 101 games.

This was the Yankee team labeled "Murderers' Row" by the fawning New York press, who relished the way the Yankees sucked the life out of opposing pitchers. Their lineup, peppered with future Hall of Fame members, terrorized the other seven American League clubs with their explosive bats. Their names, at least most of them, are still known by casual followers of the sport, even though they played in a long ago era: Gehrig, Ruth, Lazzeri, Combs, Meusel, Koenig, Dugan. Poor Johnny Grabowski, the Yankees' regular catcher in 1928, must have felt out of place, with his one solitary home run and slender .238 batting average. The other seven regulars soared above him, at least offensively. Ruth and Gehrig each had 142 runs batted in; Ruth clouted a whopping 54 home runs and Gehrig had 27. Combs led the AL with 21 triples. Gehrig led all AL batters in doubles, with 47 (Meusel, with 45, was not far behind). Ruth, Gehrig, and Combs finished one-two-three in the AL's run-scoring category. New York averaged nearly six runs scored per game, and it must have seemed like utter futility for the have-not clubs (such as Cleveland and Boston) to attempt to stop the irresistible Yankee machine.

Despite such terrific credentials to back up the Yankees' obvious claim of being baseball's best team, there were still members of the 1928 Yankees who were *underrated*: the pitching staff. Herb Pennock led the AL in shutouts in 1928 with five. George Pipgras, another New York starter, had four. Pipgras compiled 24 victories that season. Waite Hoyt won 23. Pennock was responsible for 17 wins, and Henry Johnson, the club's fourth starter, registered 14 victories. In reality, the rest of the league had the unenviable task of trying to generate offense off the AL's premier pitching staff while attempting to keep Ruth, Gehrig, Lazzeri, et al. at bay. The Philadelphia A's should be commended for just making the pennant race interesting.

Opposing the mighty Yankees in the World Series would be the St. Louis Cardinals, who two years earlier had orchestrated a storybook upset of the vaunted New Yorkers in seven heart-stopping games. It couldn't have pleased the Cards that the Yankees were openly discussing revenge for 1926 in the New York dailies, or that the 1928 Yanks were even better than the formidable foe of two seasons before. Still, there was every reason for the Cardinals to be hopeful while not being silly enough to be overly optimistic about their chances in the World Series. Four of the St. Louis regulars had batting averages of .300 or better, including Chick Hafey, who led the club with .337. Jim Bottomley, the Cardinals' talented first baseman, led the National League in two of the three major offensive categories with 31 home runs and 136 runs batted in. Pitcher Bill Sherdel won 21 of the club's 95 total victories in 1928. Jesse Haines had 20 wins. Old Grover Cleveland "Pete" Alexander, the hero of the 1926 Series, had one last prosperous season and won 16 games. Individual stars were not as plentiful on the Cardinal roster as they were in the rival Yankees' lineup, so the Cards relied on cohesive team play to win the 1928 National League flag by a two-game margin over the second-place New York Giants. Cardinals manager Bill McKechnie was fully aware that his club would need its share of breaks to once again upset the heavily favored Yankees. This time, it was not to be.

Game One, in New York City on October 4, gave a clear indication to the Cardinals why the Yankees had been so difficult to defeat all season. New York won, 4–1. Waite Hoyt tossed a complete-game three-hitter. The Yankees mustered only seven hits themselves, a poor offensive output for them, but one was a two-run homer by Bob Meusel in the home half of the fourth inning, which gave Hoyt all the support he would need. Only a solo homer in the seventh inning by Jim Bottomley prevented the Cards from being shut out. Once again, timely New York pitching secured a win when the bats were unusually silent.

In Game Two, the following afternoon, the Cardinals had scored three times against Yankee starter George Pipgras in two innings but still trailed 4–3. Cardinals starter Grover Alexander was a shell of his 1926 self, and the Yankees scored four more runs in the third inning to put the game out of reach early. Another Yankee run in the seventh capped off the scoring in a 9–3 New York win and sent the Series to St. Louis with the Cards, thoroughly frustrated, trailing two games to none.

Lou Gehrig was the star of Game Three, at Sportsman's Park in St. Louis, connecting for two home runs as the Yankees won handily by a 7–3 score. With New York leading the series 3–0, the Cardinals knew that the chance of knocking off the Yankees four straight times was remote, but the NL champions were determined to put forth one last effort to try to win a single game at least.

Game Four, on October 9, proved to be a memorable day, but alas, not for the hometown Cardinals. Bill "Wee Willie" Sherdel, the Cards' tough-luck losing pitcher in Game One, was managing to keep the Yankees in check through six innings. St. Louis was clinging to a 2–1 lead. Babe Ruth had been responsible for New York's offense to this point by swatting one of Sherdel's curveballs—one at least six inches inside—over the Sportsman's Park right-field bleachers. It had been debatable whether Ruth would even be able to play that afternoon, as he hobbled throughout the pregame warm-ups on a badly swollen ankle. But this was high drama for Ruth, and Sherdel should have taken the fourth-inning home run as a harbinger of things to come.

When Ruth came to bat in the seventh inning, Sherdel quickly got ahead of the ailing Yankee slugger with two called strikes. After the second strike, Ruth made the rookie mistake of looking up at the scoreboard without stepping out of the batter's box. This was an open invitation for Sherdel to pitch to an obviously distracted Ruth and record a cheap strikeout. Syndicated sportswriter Alan J. Gould described what happened next:

> Sherdel whipped another ball that cut the heart of the plate. It was a smart play, but [plate] umpire [Charley] Pfirman . . . had raised his palms to indicate suspension of play for the moment, as Ruth, still in the box, was obviously not in hitting position.

As far as Sherdel and the Cardinals bench were concerned, Ruth, by remaining within the batter's box, should have anticipated a pitch and was therefore liable to be struck out. Pfirman disagreed, upholding the literal interpretation of the rule which states that quick pitches are illegal and dangerous. The Cardinals tried in vain to argue that what Sherdel had done was common practice, and any batter foolish enough to be distracted while in the batter's box deserved to have a strike sail by him. Pfirman's decision to nullify Sherdel's pitch outraged the home team and divided the crowd, as Gould noted:

> Sherdel, incensed to high pitch, rushed in to protest, followed by captain [Frankie] Frisch and the rest of the Cardinals, arguing that Ruth, by remaining in the box, had been fanned. It was an angry debate, cheered on by Ruth fans' handclapping, but also to the accompaniment of wild boos and jeers from the crowd.

Ruth, thanks to the kindness of Charley Pfirman, had been given a second life at the plate. The count evened at two-and-two before he launched a tremendous drive that sailed completely over the pavilion in right field. Ruth made the most of this turn of events by mocking the crowd as he circled the bases. The game had reached its turning point. Gehrig followed with another home run. Cedric Durst added another. By the time the seventh inning had ended, Sherdel was in the showers and New York was in the lead, 5–2. Ruth was not yet finished with his heroics, however. In his final at-bat, in the eighth inning, the Bambino drove a Grover Alexander offering off the roof of the right-field pavilion for his third home run of the afternoon. Fittingly, Ruth, bad ankle and all, made the game's final putout with a sensational sliding catch in the bottom of the ninth to squelch a final St. Louis rally and cap off a spectacular 7–3 win.

The Yankees had won their second straight World Series, and had run their postseason winning streak to eight games. But was Game Four's victory tainted by the disallowed third strike which floated by Ruth in the seventh? Sherdel was clearly rattled by the incident and completely fell apart. The Yankees might well have won the game anyway, but many observers saw umpire Pfirman's actions as being overly helpful to Ruth.

According to the St. Louis argument, the rules—and standard baseball etiquette—entitled Sherdel to pitch to Ruth. After all, that was why the batter's boxes were chalked beside home plate. If a batter was stationed within the lines, he was fair game for a pitch; if he was outside of them, the pitcher had to wait until the batter was ready. Sherdel, who died in 1968, claimed for the next 42 years that he had been unfairly deprived of a strikeout by an umpire who was too protective of a batter.

But it wasn't just *a* batter, it was Babe Ruth in the batter's box, the greatest star the game has ever known. Did the Babe's fame and reputation figure into Charley Pfirman's decision to suspend play and prevent Sherdel's quick pitch? Only Pfirman knew the answer to that, but the best guess is "probably."

Chapter 9

The Stuff of Legends: Babe Ruth's "Called Shot" (1932 World Series)

> To understand him, you had to understand this: he wasn't human; he was an animal. No human could have done the things he did, lived the way he did, and been that kind of ballplayer. Cobb, could he pitch? Speaker? The rest? I saw them; there was never anybody close. When you figure the things he did, and the way he lived and the way he played, you gotta figure he was more than an animal even. There never was anyone like him. He was a god!
>
> —Joe Dugan, describing his roommate, Babe Ruth

The trouble with stories that become legends is that often they are more colorful than the truth. The factual truth can sometimes be bland. The truth, in order to make it palatable, and worth repeating, often needs some embellishment. Adolf Hitler had the right idea when he said, "The bigger the lie, the more people will believe it." Stories which combine myth and half-truths develop lives of their own. There are history textbooks circulating throughout American high schools, claiming that Abraham Lincoln wrote his poignant Gettysburg Address on the back of an envelope. Lincoln did no such thing. Many schoolchildren are under the impression that George Washington had wooden teeth. Again, this is false. It seems the quest for truth somehow becomes secondary to the quest for a good story, and falsehoods such as those about Washington and Lincoln go largely unchallenged, even by those who know better.

Not surprisingly, the history of sports is also filled with unsubstantiated rumors and myths that have etched their way into popular belief. When boxer Billy Conn died in 1993, obituary writers dutifully reported that Conn had had a comfortable points lead over Joe Louis in their famous 1941 heavyweight title fight, when Conn foolishly decided to go toe-to-toe with the Brown Bomber and was knocked out. It's a great story, but it isn't true. A check of the judges' scorecards indicates that Conn would have had to win at least one more round to secure a victory by decision. Still, the Conn myth persists and will likely continue to survive despite the best efforts of ring historians to correct this misconception.

Baseball, of course, is not exempt from this manipulation of history. Those old enough to remember Babe Herman gleefully relate the tale of a game in 1926 when he "doubled into a triple play" by passing two preceding baserunners. Any fan with a basic grasp of baserunning rules realizes this is impossible. When a preceding runner is passed, it is the *succeeding* runner who is declared out. On that day in 1926, Herman *tripled* into a *double* play when he and two teammates all ended up at third base at the same time. This story is just as wacky and wonderful as the myth, but this one is genuine. Still, the myth is virtually impossible to dispel.

Baseball's glorious history is filled with such tales, exaggerations that are concocted, reshaped, and eventually accepted as gospel by those who refuse to research the factual truth. Sadly, the two greatest myths in baseball history are both false. First is the Cooperstown myth (see chapter 1). The other is the story that Babe Ruth brazenly "called his shot," predicting with a gesture that he would hit a home run on the very next pitch in the 1932 World Series.

The legend of Babe Ruth's called shot is part and parcel of the enormous myth of Ruth himself. The Babe's larger-than-life personality, combined with his almost superhuman exploits on and off the playing field, made him the unchallenged sporting hero of his time. Joe Dugan's awe, quoted in the epigraph opening this chapter, is from a man who lived and worked with Ruth. Imagine how the public, who only read about him in the newspaper or heard of his accomplishments through rumor, must have felt about him. Babe Ruth, he can do it all, thought Joe Fan of the 1920s.

And why wouldn't he think that? Babe Ruth was a ballplayer who defied all logic. He began as a pitcher, and for six years had a record of 89–46—not bad for a fellow whose schooling in the game's finer points came at a reformatory for incorrigible boys. Suddenly, in 1919, Ed Barrow, Ruth's manager when he played for the Red Sox, discovered that Ruth was an offensive weapon and decided to maximize this talent by placing him in right field on the days he was not pitching. Ruth responded in the way legends do: he smacked 29 home runs, an unheard-of total in the days when the ball was dead and outfield walls were distant. The next season, when Red Sox owner Harry Frazee made the sport's most dubious deal and sent the Babe to the Yankees, Ruth obliterated his own record with 54 home runs. The next year, 1921, he upped it to 59. Baseball had never seen anybody like Ruth. And Ruth never saw a restaurant, a speakeasy, or a brothel he didn't like. Frequent hangovers, exhaustion, and a growing spare tire around Ruth's midsection did little to curtail the Ruth legend, as the home-run total mounted and new standards were set.

Surely, it seemed, there was nothing Ruth couldn't do. What about that game in St. Louis during the 1926 World Series, when he promised to hit a home run for a dying kid? Not only did Ruth belt *three* homers, but the ill child, Johnny Sylvester, somehow recovered his health! There was an almost magical quality about Ruth. His presence transcended the sport and his name became known throughout the world, even by those who had no idea about baseball. And there could be no doubt about Ruth's capacity to generate miracles after the 1927 season, when, with young, charging teammate Lou Gehrig threatening to surpass the Babe, Ruth put forth one last supreme effort, and launched 60 homers into the seats of American League ballparks. If Ruth wasn't in a class by himself, it certainly didn't take long to call the roll.

It was against this backdrop of superstardom, one that has not been approached since and probably never will be, that Ruth entered the 1932 World Series. Ruth, now 37 years old, was no longer the main offensive weapon of the vaunted New York Yankees. The mantle had been handed over to the man who followed Ruth in the Yankee batting order, Lou Gehrig. Ruth was always puzzled by Gehrig, a man who didn't smoke, didn't drink, refused to carouse, and always got a decent night's sleep. How Gehrig managed to perform as well as he did without the aid of gargantuan meals, the taste of liquor, or the services of prostitutes, was beyond the Babe's comprehension.

The Babe had a hunch that the 1932 World Series might be the last time he would perform in the game's premier event. The Yankees had had to struggle to win the American League pennant. The rest of the league was no longer composed of pushovers. The Philadelphia Athletics had rebuilt a formidable team in the late 1920s and had managed to interrupt the parade of Yankee pennants with three straight of their own in 1929, 1930, and 1931. In 1932, the Yankees had one last great year, winning 107 games, 13 more than Connie Mack's A's. There were signs that the Washington Senators and Detroit Tigers were also ready to challenge for the pennant in the next few seasons, so Ruth, nearing the end of the line, wanted the '32 Series to be special.

The opposition facing the Yankees that fall was to be the Chicago Cubs, a team which had last won a World Series when Teddy Roosevelt was in the White House. There was bad blood between the two clubs, an oddity for a World Series. Usually baseball's most heated rivalries are between teams in the same league, who play each other often through the emotionally draining days of a pennant race. The Yankees, though, had a beef with the Cubs. Toward the end of the season, Chicago had added Mark Koenig to its roster. Koenig, who had been the Yankees' shortstop during the glorious 1927 season, played a key role in helping the Cubs edge Pittsburgh for the National League pennant. He batted .353 in 33 games for the Cubs, yet somehow, when it came time to vote on dividing the World Series bonus money, Koenig's frugal teammates decreed he was entitled to just half a share. When word of this got into the newspapers, the Yankees were furious, and during the first two games of the World Series, played at Yankee Stadium, the Cubs' lack of generosity was the subject most discussed by the hecklers on the New York bench.

New York won the first two contests by scores of 12–6 and 5–2 in a volatile atmosphere. Acerbic insults flew between dugouts. When Ruth proclaimed the Cubs' home park, Wrigley Field, as "a cheesy looking dump" (such heresy!), there was little hope that the teams would simmer down. Game Three was scheduled for Saturday, October 1, and would feature what respected historian Donald Honig has called in *Baseball America*, "the purest moment in all of baseball mythology."

If Game Three had ended for Ruth after the top of the first inning he still would have had a tremendous day. Ruth blasted a three-run homer off Cubs starter Charlie Root, who after today would join the long list of unfortunate hurlers who have surrendered famous home runs. Gehrig hit a solo shot in the third, but after four innings the Cubs were back in the fight, having tied the score at 4–4. Ruth strode to the plate in the top of the fifth. His earlier home run had served only to infuriate the Chicago crowd further. The jeering of the Cubs' bench now merged with the razzing of fifty thousand people who wanted nothing better than to see Ruth go down on strikes. The count reached two-and-two. What happened next is arguably the most widely discussed moment in baseball history.

According to those faithful to the Ruth myth, this is what happened. After the second strike was called and the taunts of the Cubs and the crowd grew to new heights, Ruth defiantly pointed toward the centerfield bleachers, leaving no doubt that was where he intended to deposit the next pitch. Let history record that the next pitch sailed well over the center-field fence and, said Chicago sportswriters, was the longest ball ever hit at Wrigley Field. Ruth, living up to his legend, had apparently kept his word and called his shot.

Many of Ruth's teammates stood by this story as it was repeated over the years. "I was in the ballgame," stated Joe Sewell. "I saw it all, saw every bit of it. Don't let anybody tell you that he did not point to the fence. He did!" Oddly enough, for such a momentous event, only one New York reporter noted it in the next day's accounts of the game. John Drebinger of *The New York Times* said

Ruth had indeed called his shot, but only noted it well into his story. Everything that Ruth did on the field was recorded in meticulous detail by the New York writers. It seems unbelievable that so many could have overlooked such a supposedly dramatic moment.

Another writer, Joe Williams of the Scripps-Howard newspapers, made the most of Ruth's gesture, whatever it was, and the story of the "called shot" received syndicated coverage through his report. Only after Williams' story got back to New York did the majority of that city's writers "remember" what Ruth had supposedly done. Charlie Root, the Chicago pitcher who probably had the best vantage point, was adamant—Ruth did not point. "If he had made a gesture like that," said Root and quoted in *Baseball Anecdotes*, "he would have ended up on his ass." There is little doubting Root, who had the reputation of being one of the surliest pitchers in the majors, and was known to respond to showmanship with a fastball aimed at the head. Yankees manager Joe McCarthy, who did not particularly like Ruth, was quoted in *Baseball America* as stating, "I didn't see him point anywhere at all." But he added, "I might have turned my head for a moment."

The Yankees won Game Three 7–5, and Game Four the next day 13–6, to sweep the Cubs. Gehrig did most of the offensive damage in the series, but that single plate appearance of Ruth's in the fifth inning of Game Three transcended anything anybody else did. Ruth himself played the story for all it was worth, adding incorrect details (such as the count being oh-and-two). It all added to the Ruth legend, and, of course, Ruth favored this. A great many witnesses concede that Ruth held up his hand before the fateful pitch, but many state he was just indicating that he still had one more strike left. Others go all the way. Babe Ruth, being Babe Ruth, did the improbable, and called his shot.

If there was any doubt that the "called shot" was nothing more then embellished hyperbole, it was put to rest one day in 1942 on a Hollywood movie set. MGM was filming *The Pride of the Yankees*, a biography of Lou Gehrig. Babe Herman and Babe Ruth both had roles in the film and were relaxing during a break in shooting when Charlie Root came strolling onto the set. Root and Ruth had never formally met, and were quickly introduced by Herman. Root got to the point in short order. "You never pointed out to center field before you hit that ball off of me, did you?" he asked Ruth.

"I know I didn't," chuckled Ruth. "But it made a hell of a story, didn't it?"

That was the truth, according to witness Babe Herman. Nevertheless, baseball writer Roger Kahn summed it up best:

> The stories are marvelous. Let them roll on. You don't always need truth. You don't always need absolute accuracy. Let the story be: Ruth called his shot. I'm pleased with that.

The Babe, wherever he is now, would be pleased, too.

Chapter 10

The Goat and the Hero: Johnny Pesky Holds the Ball as Enos Slaughter Scores (1946 World Series)

When it comes to remembering sports figures, the public's taste generally runs in extremes. Fans usually have little trouble recalling the immortals who performed feats which have stood the test of time. Good examples of this are Jack Dempsey roaring back to win a heavyweight title fight after being knocked through the ropes; the famous Four Horsemen of Notre Dame, who led Knute Rockne's school to the 1924 national collegiate football championship; the 1980 U.S. Olympic hockey team winning an unexpected gold medal in Lake Placid; and many more. Spectacular losers also come to mind. Billy Conn getting knocked out by Joe Louis when it seemed the handsome Irishman had the heavyweight title locked up; the 1976 Tampa Bay Buccaneers, who went 0–14 in their first NFL season; and perhaps even the pitiful 11 law students who comprised the 1916 Cumberland College football squad—a team that dropped a game to mighty Georgia Tech 222–0.

Major-league baseball, in its 120 years of history, has, of course, produced its share of spectacular heroes. Babe Ruth's accomplishments have filled books; Bobby Thomson, some four decades after he hit the sport's most famous home run, is still in demand by autograph seekers; the image of Kirk Gibson, hobbling around the basepaths at Dodger Stadium after launching an improbable World Series homer, is firmly etched in a corner of our minds. Conversely, baseball has produced some of sport's most famous losers. When one thinks of Bobby Thomson, one almost naturally thinks of Brooklyn pitcher Ralph Branca, off whom Thomson homered. Likewise, Dennis Eckersley, despite his years of bullpen brilliance, will probably be remembered 70 years from now as the unfortunate soul who dished up Gibson's home run.

Given the intense scrutiny under which the World Series is played each October, the deeds or misdeeds of players are magnified. Bill Mazeroski is forever a hero for his dramatic home run in the bottom of the ninth inning in Game Seven of the 1960 World Series. Don Larsen, whose career was mediocre at best, has a hallowed name because he happened to pitch a perfect game in the 1956 World Series, a feat that has not been duplicated (and perhaps never will be). Unfortunately, blunders receive just as much publicity as World Series heroics, and the label "World Series goat" can be a burdensome one indeed. The first acknowledged World Series goat was probably Fred Snodgrass of the New York Giants, who, in the dying moments of the 1912 World Series, allowed a routine fly ball to elude him and cost his talented club the Series. Fans have long memories, and Snodgrass' blunder has been told and retold to younger generations of baseball fans. When Snodgrass died in 1974, his obituary in the *New York Times* ran under the headline "Old Ballplayer Snodgrass Dies; Dropped Fly Ball in 1912."

Hank Gowdy, the New York Giants' catcher in the 1924 World Series, had a similar disaster befall him. In the late innings of Game Seven against Washington, Gowdy attempted to catch a routine foul pop-up, only to be sabotaged by his own discarded mask! Gowdy, while looking skyward, caught his foot in his mask and could not chase down what should have been an easy out. The batter, Muddy Ruel, given a second chance, got a key hit, enabling the Senators to win the game.

Mickey Owen of the Brooklyn Dodgers might very well be the most famous of World Series goats for not catching a third strike thrown by pitcher Hugh Casey. If Owen had caught the pitch (which many suspect was a wicked spitball), the Dodgers would have evened the 1941 World Series at two games apiece with the crosstown Yankees. Instead, the Yankees hitter, Tommy Henrich, reached first base and began a rally which enabled the Yankees to win the game and take a 3–1 lead in the Series. Not surprisingly, the defeat was shattering to the Dodgers, who never recovered psychologically from being so close to levelling the series. They lost the next day and the Yankees won the 1941 World Series in five games.

Other noteworthy—but perhaps underserving—goats come to mind as well. Remember Cincinnati's big catcher Ernie Lombardi "snoozing" at home plate as Joe DiMaggio scored the Series-winning run in 1940? Most people forget that Lombardi had been flattened by a collision earlier on the play and was clearly groggy. And let us not forget Boston's much-maligned Bill Buckner, who allowed a Mookie Wilson dribbler to go through his legs in the tenth inning of Game Six of the 1986 World Series. It is often overlooked that Buckner was badly hobbling throughout the Series, and with the Red Sox holding the lead, manager John McNamara should have replaced the ailing Buckner with a more competent and healthier first baseman.

Superstars are also handed the "goat" label for not producing as expected in World Series play. Ted Williams was a bust in his only World Series appearance, going 5-for-25 at the plate, all five hits being singles. Dave Winfield had but one hit in 22 plate appearances for the Yankees in 1981. Oakland's José Canseco and Mark McGwire were both spectacular flops in 1988, batting .053 and .059 respectively. Ty Cobb played in three World Series and did not come close to matching the offensive numbers one might expect from baseball's best pure hitter.

Most players who have received the "goat" label, both superstars and those known only to devoted followers of box scores, deserve it. But one man, Boston Red Sox shortstop Johnny Pesky, has improperly been accused of costing his club the 1946 World Series. The charge is that he made a mental miscue, holding on to the ball too long and allowing St. Louis Cardinals runner Enos Slaughter to scamper home with the Series-deciding run. This is blatantly unfair to Pesky. It is also a discredit to Slaughter, who should be lauded for his aggressive baserunning and skillful reading of the play. In other words, there was no goat, as has been widely suggested, but there was indeed a hero, which has often been ignored.

The 1946 season was just a combination of the success the St. Louis Cardinals had experienced during the war years. While other clubs floundered when the military draft decimated their rosters, the Cardinals managed to excel. The Redbirds won the National League pennant in 1942 and defeated the Yankees in the World Series that October.

The Cards repeated as NL titleholders in 1943, but this time lost to the Yanks in the Fall Classic. St. Louis made it three straight pennants in 1944 and claimed the world championship by beating their crosstown rivals, the AL champion St. Louis Browns, in six games in the one and only all–St. Louis World Series. The Chicago Cubs ended the Cardinals' reign atop the NL standings in 1945, but St. Louis defeated the feisty Brooklyn Dodgers to regain NL honors in 1946. It was not easy, however. Both the Cardinals and the Dodgers finished the season in a dead heat, and a best-two-out-of-three playoff series—the first ever in major league baseball—was needed before the Cards emerged as the league's champions for the fourth time in five seasons.

The Red Sox had experienced no such success during the war, or in the 20 years which preceded the global conflict. Boston's last American League pennant had come in 1918, when the Allies were battling Kaiser Wilhelm rather than Adolf Hitler. By the early 1930s, the Red Sox could be found at the bottom of the AL standings. The emergence of a young California hitting machine named Ted Williams gave hope to the Fenway faithful when he arrived in Boston for the 1939 season. In the magical year of 1941, when American youth was still uninvolved in the World War, Williams fulfilled all of his potential, batting .406 to win the AL batting crown and becoming perhaps baseball's last .400 hitter. Still, the Red Sox went without a pennant. In 1941 the Yankees, inspired by Joe DiMaggio's astonishing 56-game hitting streak, ran away with the AL flag, leaving Boston 17 games back in second place. Even Williams capturing the elusive Triple Crown in 1942 could not turn Boston into a championship club. The Air Force then called Williams, who spent the next three seasons flying combat missions instead of hitting baseballs. Without "the Kid," as Williams was known to Boston fans, the Red Sox had no hope of breaking the skein of pennantless summers.

Then the war ended. Williams and his batting eye returned to Boston. All was right with the world. The Red Sox seemed to return to form before the other AL clubs, and Boston won the 1946 AL flag. The oddsmakers, dismissing the Cardinals' past successes as a wartime fluke, installed the Red Sox as heavy 20–7 favorites as the 1946 World Series opened at Sportsman's Park in St. Louis. Game One seemed to be a positive omen for Red Sox fans. Trailing 2–1 in the top of the ninth, Boston scored the tying run when a routine ground ball took a peculiar hop through Cardinals shortstop Marty Marion's legs. A Rudy York home run in the top of the tenth provided the margin of victory as the Red Sox won 3–2 to open the Series.

St. Louis' Harry Brecheen, who would shine as the pitching star of the series, held Boston to just four hits in Game Two as the Cards won, 3–0. For the next three contests the series shifted to Boston, where the long-suffering fans hoped the Red Sox could win their first World Series since the days of Babe Ruth. York's three-run homer in the first inning, plus shutout pitching by Boo Ferriss, gave Boston a 4–0 win in Game Three. But any thoughts of an easy Boston triumph quickly vanished in Game Four as St. Louis routed the Red Sox, 12–3. Six Boston pitchers were required to retire the Cardinals hitters in the one-sided affair. Pivotal Game Five went to Boston, 6–3, as Joe Dobson hurled a complete game for the home side. Fenway Park would not host another World Series game for 21 years.

One game away from defeat, St. Louis rallied in Game Six. Harry Brecheen was once again brilliant on the mound for the Cardinals, pitching a complete-game, 4–1 victory. A seventh game would be necessary to decide the World Series champions of 1946. The usual sellout crowd was present on Monday, October 15, at Sportsman's Park to witness the affair in which Johnny Pesky would gain everlasting notoriety and Enos Slaughter would make a famous trip around the basepaths.

After seven innings, it looked as if St. Louis would complete their comeback without much challenge. The Cardinals led 3–1 and pitcher Murry Dickson appeared to have the Bosox under his control. The Red Sox refused to capitulate, however, and stormed back to score two runs in the top of the eighth. Harry Brecheen, the winning pitcher two days earlier, had to be summoned from the bullpen to stifle the Boston rally. He did, and the top of the eighth ended with the score knotted at 3–3. Bob Klinger was pitching for the Red Sox in the bottom of the eighth. Enos Slaughter, the Cardinals' hard-playing outfielder, led off with a single. Two batters failed to produce anything, and Slaughter remained fixed at first base with two outs. Harry Walker was the next St. Louis batter. In the dugout, manager Eddie Dyer signalled for the hit-and-run play. As Klinger delivered to Walker, Slaughter broke for second base. Walker connected for a soft line drive which fell into shallow center field in front of outfielder Leon Culberson. Associated Press reporter Jack Hand described what happened next:

> [Slaughter] catapulted off first base, rounded second and headed for third while Culberson . . . made a quick relay to shortstop Johnny Pesky.
>
> Making the full sweep at third while coach Mike Gonzalez signalled the come-on sign, Slaughter sprinted for the plate.
>
> Pesky, apparently not expecting that sort of daring baserunning, had dropped his arm halfway, watching Walker run toward second, before he realized Slaughter was hotfooting home with the tie-breaking run. His peg to [catcher] Ray Partee was too late as Slaughter topped off his magnificent heads-up running with a fine slide that scored a run.

Walker's hit, which was scored a double, had brought home Enos Slaughter. The run made it a 4–3 game. Boston tried to rally in the top of the ninth, but came up short. St. Louis held on to their lead and won the series. Almost immediately, Pesky was labeled a goat for allowing Slaughter to score virtually unchallenged. Among the first to come to Pesky's defense was Slaughter himself. To this day, Slaughter feels that

> Pesky got hit with a bum rap.... Because of the steal sign, I already had a pretty good jump on the pitcher when Walker hit this little floater into center field. The play was in front of me, so I could easily see that nobody was going to catch the ball. In fact, the ball was still in the air when I came into second base. I knew third base was a cinch and I began to think I might make it all the way, especially since I knew that Culberson was not a strong thrower.
>
> Pesky had to go out to take the outfielder's throw, and he couldn't see me, what with his back to the plate. It was up to his teammates to yell to him, but nobody did. You couldn't blame Pesky. By the time he turned around and got ready to throw, I was just a step or two away from the plate.
>
> —*The World Series*

In what became known as "Slaughter's mad dash," Pesky was named as a villain who choked at the thought of firing the ball home. Films of the play show that Slaughter was safe by a huge margin. Partee had to come up the line to take Pesky's throw. In all likelihood, even a perfect throw would not have gotten Slaughter at the plate.

Nevertheless, Pesky was blamed for costing the Red Sox the 1946 World Series title. His alleged miscue was discussed with the same disdain as Mickey Owen's passed ball and Fred Snodgrass' dropped fly ball. Although defended by Slaughter and his Red Sox teammates, Pesky was reviled as the man who cost Boston the World Series, mainly by those who weren't present at Sportsman's Park and were basing their judgment solely on hearsay.

No matter where he went, Pesky could not escape the taunts of the legions of Red Sox fans who believed he was the sole reason why St. Louis had won the World Series instead of Boston. That November, Pesky was present at a football game at the University of Washington and was introduced to the crowd by the public-address announcer. As the football game progressed, it turned into a sloppy affair marred by fumble after fumble. Finally, a heckler shouted from the stands, "Give the ball to Pesky. He'll hold on to it!"

Chapter 11

Starting for the Red Sox Is . . . Denny Galehouse? (1948)

> McCarthy pinned the Boston fortunes on the tired right arm of Denny Galehouse, a 36-year-old journeyman in the twilight of a mediocre career.
>
> —*The Baseball Hall of Shame 2*
> (Bruce Nash and Allan Zullo)

The name of Joe McCarthy, to most baseball followers, is forever linked with the glorious New York Yankee clubs of the 1930s. McCarthy had the distinct privilege of piloting the powerful Yankees for 16 seasons, from 1931 to 1946. Ruth, Gehrig, DiMaggio, Dickey, Gomez, and a supporting cast of lesser greats wore the pinstripes with McCarthy at the helm. McCarthy led his club to World Series victories in 1932, 1936, 1937, 1938, 1939, 1941, and 1943. (The Yanks also won the American League pennant in 1942, but—horror of horrors—actually lost in the World Series.) Truly, McCarthy was blessed with great players. Still, many managers have had great players and yet faltered when expected to win. If a good manager is one who gets the most out of the players on his roster, McCarthy (like Casey Stengel after him) must be considered one of the sport's giants.

If you happen to be a fan of the Boston Red Sox, the name Joe McCarthy doesn't necessarily evoke the same memories of managerial greatness. McCarthy, after being dumped by the Yankee hierarchy 35 games into the 1946 season for the high crime of being in second place, was hired to lead the resurgent Boston Red Sox beginning in the 1948 season. This he did for two and one-half seasons. In both 1948 and 1949, the Red Sox had better-than-legitimate chances to capture the American League pennant. They failed on both occasions. In 1949, the Bosox needed one win in their final two games at Yankee Stadium to capture the flag. The Yankees won both crucial contests and the American League pennant. This was heartbreaking but acceptable to the Fenway fans. The Red Sox had fought valiantly and played their best, but had lost to a terrific New York club that was just a bit better than Boston when it really counted.

The events of the previous year, 1948, were not as easy to swallow for the Red Sox fans. Their beloved club had rallied in the closing days of the schedule to catch the front-running Cleveland Indians, who appeared to have a lock on the AL pennant. Boston and Cleveland ended the schedule in a tie, the first time such an occurrence had been seen in the 48-year history of the American League. The Indians and the Red Sox would decide the championship with a dramatic one-game playoff. The winner would meet the National League champions, the Boston Braves, in the opening game of the World Series two days later. McCarthy's decision to use wornout, fading veteran Denny Galehouse as his starting pitcher in that playoff game has perplexed Red Sox fans for more than four decades.

The 1948 season came at the beginning of what baseball historians refer to as the golden age of the sport. The Second World War had devastated major-league rosters for the better part of four seasons. Most able-bodied players had enlisted or been drafted into the armed forces for the duration of the war. Those who remained in the big leagues were either beyond their primes and of no use to the military, incapacitated in some way, or, in a few extreme cases, too young to serve their country. Naturally, the quality of play deteriorated badly. The absolute nadir was reached at the end of the 1945 season, when the Detroit Tigers and the Chicago Cubs bungled their way through a truly terrible World Series, one which a reporter, quoted in *Baseball Anecdotes*, described as "some of the worst-played baseball games at the major-league level." Routine fly balls often became an adventure. Inept pitching squared off against incompetent hitting. If this was the World Series, supposedly baseball's showcase event, one can just imagine how lousy the caliber of play was in the low minor leagues during the war years. It is a testament to the enduring appeal of the sport that baseball managed to survive these lean years and retain its fan appeal.

Normalcy returned with the spring of 1946. Reality entered the picture in 1947, when the Brooklyn Dodgers dared to write Jackie Robinson's name on their roster, making Robinson the first black player to compete at the major-league level in 63 seasons. Cleveland's Larry Doby integrated the American League in 1948, and the longstanding color barrier became a thing of the past, although pioneers such as Robinson found out the transition was not a smooth one. Baseball was booming once again, especially in Cleveland, where the pennant-contending Indians were attracting enormous crowds to brand-new Municipal Stadium. Owner Bill Veeck, a promotional genius, used a combination of weird enticement and a talented team to keep the turnstiles rotating in a city that was not used to a pennant possibility. By the end of the 1948 season, the Indians had drawn more than two and a half million spectators, an impressive number today but an utterly fantastic figure in 1948, when day games were still commonplace. The orchids, the cars, and the razor blades that Veeck gave away to the Cleveland fans were nice, but the genuine attraction at Municipal Stadium during the summer of 1948 was the Indians and their riveting battle against the AL's two most glamorous clubs, the Red Sox and the Yankees.

As September reached its midpoint, the nation's sportswriters began to search their vocabularies to describe the exciting pennant race in which Cleveland, Boston, and New York were engulfed. There hadn't been a serious three-team race in the AL since the 1908 campaign, when both the White Sox and the Indians finished within a game of Detroit. A casual fan who failed to check the American League standings each evening could become woefully out of touch with the leapfrogging which seemed to be occurring from day to day. The Red Sox held a one-game lead on September 22. On

September 23, the Red Sox and Indians were tied for the lead, thanks to a 5–2 Cleveland victory over Boston. By September 25, the Yankees had climbed back into contention and all three contenders were now tied, with identical records of 91–56.

Already the thought that the 154-game schedule would not be sufficient to decide the AL flag was occurring to those who mattered. On September 28, Cleveland's player-manager Lou Boudreau announced that if a one-game playoff were necessary he would likely use Bob Lemon as his starter. Boudreau was a happy man that day, as Cleveland crept into a one-game lead over both Boston and New York. On September 29, the Indians' lead grew to two full games, with just four dates left on each club's schedule. Full of confidence, Boudreau told the Associated Press, "Nothing short of a major catastrophe can stop us now. The boys are hitting. The morale is high. There is no sign of jitters." Boudreau's confidence seemed well founded, especially after each club won its next game, leaving Cleveland with a two-game lead with only three games left.

The final weekend of the 1948 AL schedule approached. Cleveland's lead shrank to one game after they unexpectedly lost to Detroit at home by a 5–3 score and Boston and New York both won crucial games. Saturday, October 2, saw the Yankees eliminated from the race after suffering a 5–1 loss to the Red Sox at Fenway. Cleveland defeated Detroit 8–0 to retain its tenuous one-game lead over the Red Sox. The Red Sox would have to beat the Yankees again on Sunday and hope that the Indians would falter against Detroit. If both these results happened, the Red Sox and Indians would finish in a first-place tie. Cleveland, noticeably nervous, lost badly to Detroit, 7–1. Boston, seizing the opportunity to force a playoff, walloped New York 10–5 before a delighted hometown crowd. For the first time in American League history, a one-game, sudden-death playoff game would have to be played. By a prearranged settlement, it would be held at Fenway Park in Boston. The Red Sox were delighted. They were hot and Cleveland was reeling. When asked whom he would use as a starting pitcher, Boston manager Joe McCarthy was quoted by the Associated Press as saying, "I had everybody working in the bullpen this afternoon and I haven't the ghost of an idea who I'll start tomorrow." Mel Parnell, Boston's ace lefty, went home and confided to his wife that he would be pitching the biggest game of his life on Monday afternoon.

Meanwhile, Boudreau had altered his earlier plans and said that Gene Bearden would throw for his club on October 4. Who the Boston pitcher would be was still a mystery. Associated Press reporter Ralph Roden speculated, "Best guess is that either Ellis Kinder or Mel Parnell will work for the Red Sox," adding, almost as an afterthought, "with Denny Galehouse as a dark horse." One can understand the reporter's reluctance to even consider the possibility of McCarthy opting for Galehouse. The Marshallville, Ohio, native was nearing his thirty-seventh birthday, and had struggled through the 1948 season to an 8–8 record. His earned-run average was nothing spectacular (4.00), and he had struck out only 38 batters in 137.1 innings. Galehouse's past was also less than legendary. His most productive season had been with the St. Louis Browns in 1942, when he had won 12 games. He had also lost 12 games in 1942. Surely, with Kinder and Parnell available, young, and healthy, Galehouse would be only a spectator on October 4.

As was his custom, Galehouse arrived early at Fenway Park on Monday. Fully expecting not to play, he dressed in his uniform and began a rigorous workout in the outfield, chasing fly balls. A clubhouse attendant approached Galehouse and told him that manager McCarthy wished to see him. Galehouse figured McCarthy would tell him to be ready in case he was needed as an emergency reliever. Galehouse was totally unprepared for McCarthy's stunning announcement: he would be the starting pitcher. The entire pennant hopes of the Red Sox were resting on him. Years later, Parnell recalled, "Denny went white as a ghost."

Realizing that his robust fly-chasing had sapped him of his usual energy, Galehouse began frantically warming up in the Red Sox bullpen. When Cleveland player-manager Lou Boudreau was told that Galehouse was preparing to pitch, he could not believe it. In fact, he thought it was a ruse concocted by McCarthy. Boudreau was convinced that either Kinder or Parnell was secretly loosening up in a secluded area and Galehouse was acting as a decoy. Only when the lineup cards were exchanged at home plate before the game and Galehouse was listed as Boston's pitcher did Boudreau finally accept the fact that McCarthy was going to use his fading veteran to start this critical game.

If McCarthy had hoped to inspire Galehouse to pitch the game of his life, he learned very early in the game that it would not happen. Boudreau, still amazed at McCarthy's pitching selection, homered off Galehouse in the top of the first inning to put Cleveland ahead 1–0. Boston managed to even the score, and Galehouse, laboring with each toss, kept Cleveland at bay through three innings. As the Indians prepared to bat in the top of the fourth, Galehouse simply ran out of gas and the roof caved in on Boston. Ken Keltner, the Cleveland third baseman, smashed a three-run homer to break the game wide open. Galehouse was finished, and McCarthy knew it. He had given up four runs on eight hits. Boudreau homered again, to give Cleveland a huge 5–1 lead, a lead it would never relinquish. The Indians went on to win 8–3 and earn a spot in the 1948 World Series against the Boston Braves.

As expected, the Red Sox fans were furious with McCarthy for starting Galehouse. A loss to Cleveland would have been bearable if Boston had gone with one if its top starters. Parnell was 15–8, Kinder was 10–7. Two other Boston starters, Joe Dobson and Jack Kramer, also had impressive records in 1948, going 16–10 and 18–5, respectively. "With everything riding on the game, it didn't make a lot of sense [to start Galehouse]," said Parnell, who was quoted in *The Baseball Hall of Shame*.

Galehouse returned to the Red Sox lineup for the 1949 season, and this time there was virtually nothing left in his arm. He hurled a grand total of two innings in two relief appearances, allowing three earned runs, for an embarrassing ERA of 13.50. He left major-league baseball with a career record of 109 wins and 118 losses. He would certainly be a forgotten name from baseball's past if one of those losses hadn't been recorded at Fenway Park on October 4, 1948.

Cleveland made the most of its World Series appearance, winning in six games against the Braves, to capture its most recent world championship. The Yankees returned to dominance in the American League in 1949, edging out the Red Sox in another dramatic pennant race. The 1949 season marked the first of five consecutive AL pennants for New York (not to mention five straight World Series titles, too). Only twice from 1949 through 1964 would the Yankees *not* win the American League championship. Cleveland would break through in 1954 and Chicago in 1959. Other than those two freak occurrences, the Yankees owned the American League.

For the Red Sox, who had come so close, an American League pennant would not fly in Boston again until 1967. By that time, Joe McCarthy was a retired old man in Buffalo, New York, Ellis Kinder was dying in Tennessee, the Braves were in Atlanta, and baseball no longer held a nation in its grip as it once did. The Red Sox lost the 1967 World Series in seven games, just as they would the 1975 and 1986 World Series. Always one step short, one hurdle away from baseball's ultimate prize. Each of those seasons had its lost opportunities, but none stood out so clearly as in 1948, when the Red Sox had the chance to put away a depressed Cleveland team and failed, largely because of one of the most perplexing managerial maneuvers ever made in a critical situation—McCarthy choosing to start Galehouse. Mel Parnell was right. It didn't make a lot of sense.

Chapter 12

Bob Feller's Pickoff Play: Runner Caught Off Base, Ump Caught Off Guard (1948 World Series)

> Be not afraid of greatness: some are born great, some achieve greatness, and some have greatness thrust upon 'em.
>
> —Shakespeare, *Twelfth Night*

Pitching greatness, for any fan lucky enough to have followed the sport in the 1930s and 1940s, was defined by Bob Feller, a young lad from the farming area of Van Meter, Iowa, who simply dared hitters in the American League to try to hit his blazing fastball. Not many succeeded on a regular basis. He was born to greatness; that, is he was born to pitch. The locals around Van Meter knew it. The stories of Feller whiffing grown men while just a boy were part of the lore that surrounded the big right-hander. If his family's barn had eyes it would have witnessed the seemingly endless hours of Robert firing his heater to his father, who was certain his son was destined for the major leagues. That barn also would have seen his father suffer some broken ribs one afternoon when he misjudged one of his boy's pitches, which crashed into his unprotected chest. The barn if it had human emotions, would have grimaced on more than one occasion, when an errant toss by Feller smashed through the lumber which acted as a makeshift backstop in these daily practice sessions.

The young hitters in the American Legion games in which Feller displayed his talent were simply overmatched. Among the most impressed observers were the league's umpires, who took it upon themselves to write to Cleveland Indians scout Cy Slapnicka and insist that a trip to see young Robert Feller pitch would be money well spent. Slapnicka did go, and left the park convinced that Feller was the greatest raw talent ever to step onto a pitcher's mound. He reported his find to the Cleveland management, who were naturally skeptical but were willing to give the unknown farm boy a shot. With a contract calling for $75 a month (plus a bonus of one dollar and an autographed ball!) Feller established himself in Cleveland, although the club's braintrust was reluctant to actually use him in a real game. After all, this was the summer of 1936, and Bob Feller was only 17.

On July 6, 1936, the All-Star break stopped the major league schedule and allowed the clubs to participate in exhibition games and test their rookies. The St. Louis Cardinals arrived in Cleveland with most of their regulars—the squad which had won the World Series just a year and a half before. Slapnicka used this opportunity to plead with Indians manager Steve O'Neill to let Feller pitch a couple of innings. At first, O'Neill thought Slapnicka was insane for thinking a teenager could compete with such a great array of stars. But since Slapnicka was adamant, O'Neill agreed to let Feller pitch three innings. It was the first opportunity big league fans got to look at a young man who was born to pitch. Feller had a unique windup: a deep forward bend, a grand sweeping motion of his arms, and a high kick of his left leg—a motion which would soon be emulated by those who wished to be like him. In those three innings, the Feller legend was born. The talented St. Louis lineup managed just two bloop hits while striking out eight times. The kid was for real and Slapnicka was not exaggerating about the potential in him. Dizzy Dean, the legendary Cardinals pitcher, was thoroughly impressed. When asked after the game if he would pose for a photograph with the young Cleveland prodigy, *Baseball America* quotes Dean as remarking, "You'd better ask him if he'll pose with me!"

Still, there were naysayers. The eight strikeouts against the Cardinals came in an exhibition game, they said. Let's see if this youngster can duplicate his efforts in a genuine American League game. Manager O'Neill must have been one of those doubters, for he waited until August 23 to test his phenom in a real game. In that start, versus the St. Louis Browns, Feller exceeded all expectations by striking out 15 batters, one shy of the AL record and two short of Dizzy Dean's NL mark. Emmett Ormsby, who umpired that historic game and had been working AL games since 1923, declared that Feller was faster than Lefty Grove or Walter Johnson, no doubt about it. In his first season with Cleveland, Feller posted a 5–3 record. One of those wins came against the Philadelphia Athletics on September 13. On that day Feller struck out 17 A's. There was absolutely no doubt that Cy Slapnicka had not been exaggerating.

With maturity, Feller became even more dominant. He won 24 games in 1939, leading the AL. Twenty-seven wins followed in 1940. Twenty-five more came in 1941. The Second World War interrupted this great streak. Feller enlisted in the armed forces and served in some of the bloodiest battles in the Pacific. When he returned, he posted 26 wins in 1946 and another 20 in 1947. Upon retiring after the 1956 campaign, Feller had totalled 266 career victories. Undoubtedly, the total would have reached 300 if it hadn't been for the war. Truly, Feller was one of the all-time greats of the mound. However, there was something missing from his career: a World Series win. He did play on a World Series winner in 1948, but he lost both games in that particular series. Many of Feller's admirers maintain to this day that his loss in Game One of the 1948 World Series should have an asterisk beside it, thanks to what appeared to be a bad call which allowed the Boston Braves to score a tainted run and earn a controversial win.

If Bob Feller had a fault, it was that he was not pitching for the New York Yankees. If he had been part of New York's starting rotation, he would have been a regular fixture in the World Series. Feller's career ran concurrently with the Yankees' total domination of the American League. Feller first pitched for the Indians in 1936.

In that same year, the Yankees won the first of four straight AL pennants (perhaps the arrival of Joe DiMaggio in 1936 had something to do with it). From 1936 to 1939, Feller's Indians could finish no better than third in what must have seemed a futile battle to catch the all-powerful New Yorkers. The Yankees faltered in 1940, ending up in third place, two games in back of Detroit. Cleveland came in second, one game ahead of New York, but one crucial game behind the frontrunning Tigers. New York returned to form in 1941, Feller's last full season before the war, making a mockery of the pennant race, finishing 17 full games ahead of Boston. Cleveland was well back in fourth place, 26 games in arrears. When Feller returned in 1946, he was about the only bright spot in the Cleveland lineup as the Indians came in sixth. The tribe improved to fourth in 1947, and only the most optimistic Cleveland rooter would have predicted a pennant-winning season for 1948.

The American League in 1948 saw perhaps its best pennant race ever. Three clubs (Cleveland, Boston, and New York) staged a dramatic run for the pennant. When the regular season ended, nothing had been decided. The Red Sox and the Indians finished in a tie for first with identical 96–58 records. New York was not far back, with 94 wins. For the first time in that league's history, a one-game playoff would be required to determine which club would play the Boston Braves in the upcoming World Series. Cleveland won the playoff 8–3 to negate the possibility of an all–Boston Fall Classic, largely due to Red Sox manager Joe McCarthy's peculiar decision to start over-the-hill Denny Galehouse in this most critical game (see chapter 11). The playoff game victory meant that for the first time since 1920, the Cleveland Indians would be appearing in a World Series.

Their opponents, the Boston Braves, weren't exactly loaded with World Series experience either, having last played in baseball's premier event in 1914. For many of the 34 seasons in between, the Braves had been the designated patsies of the National League, often wallowing at or near the bottom of the standings. In 1947, under manager Billy Southworth, the Braves had finished a respectable third, and in 1948 cruised home in first place, six games ahead of the St. Louis Cardinals. As the 1948 World Series began, baseball fans were having the unusual experience of seeing two perennial losing clubs battle it out for absolute supremacy. Fans of Bob Feller, realizing that this might be his only chance at performing in a World Series, eagerly awaited Game One at Braves Field, where Feller was penciled in as Cleveland's starting pitcher.

Amid the threat of heavy rain, the Braves and Indians took the field on Wednesday, October 6. Opposing Feller that afternoon was Johnny Sain, who had teamed with Warren Spahn that summer to stymie the rest of the National League. "Spahn and Sain and pray for rain!" was the rallying cry of Braves fans in 1948. It wasn't an entirely fair comment, considering that the twosome had combined for just 39 of Boston's 91 victories. Bill Voiselle had won 13 games and Vern Bickford had won 11. Still, Sain and Spahn were recognized as the heart of the Braves' pitching staff, and Billy Southworth was counting on Sain to win the first game. After all, the oddsmakers had listed Cleveland as an 11–5 favorite to win the Series, and Boston believed they needed a victory in Game One to establish that they indeed had a chance.

A team of six umpires was assigned to work the 1948 World Series, three from each league. Cleveland's player-manager Lou Boudreau talked to the crew prior to the first game. He wanted to point out to the three National League umpires (Bill Stewart, Babe Pinelli, and George Barr) that the Indians had developed quite an effective pickoff play at second base, and he wanted to be certain that the NL umps, who hadn't seen it, would be alert for it when the time came. The crew told Boudreau not to worry; they weren't going to be fooled. In private, Bill Stewart, working his third World Series, indignantly complained about Boudreau's concern. He had never been caught off guard on a pickoff play before, no matter how ingenious. Why would he be caught today? This complacency would come back to haunt both Stewart and the Cleveland Indians.

Sain and Feller did not disappoint those who came to Braves Field expecting a classic pitchers' duel. After seven and a half innings, the score was still 0–0. Cleveland had managed just four hits off Sain. Feller was doing even better: Boston had just one hit. Despite two Cleveland errors, the Braves had been blanked from the scoresheet. Bill Salkeld, Boston's catcher, led off the bottom of the eighth. He raised the hopes of the hometown fans by drawing a walk from Feller. Manager Southworth, sensing that this might be Boston's only scoring opportunity, replaced Salkeld with pinch runner Phil Masi. Masi moved to second base on Frank McCormick's sacrifice bunt. Eddie Stanky was intentionally walked to set up a potential double play. Next up was Johnny Sain. Southworth opted to let Sain bat for himself, but did replace Stanky at first base with another pinch runner, Sibby Sisti. Sain flied out for out number two, but Cleveland was not yet out of the woods. The next batter was Tommy Holmes, one of the National League's most reliable hitters. Boudreau, playing shortstop for Cleveland, figured it was time to try their sneaky pickoff play. Using a prearranged signal, Boudreau touched his knee as Masi took a long leadoff. Instantly, Feller wheeled around and threw toward second base. Boudreau timed the play perfectly, catching the ball and slapping it on Masi's shoulder as he slid into the bag. The fans groaned at first, certain that Masi would be called out and the rally would end. Their moans turned to cheers in a split second when second-base umpire Bill Stewart, completely fooled by Feller's move, called Masi safe.

Boudreau didn't have to move very far to argue. He slammed the ball into his glove and began questioning Stewart. Of course, Stewart wasn't going to change his call, but Boudreau wanted to let off some steam. He was convinced his tag had beaten Masi to the bag and had ended the Braves' threat. Not so, said Stewart, and the inning continued. Masi, a little wiser, stayed much closer to the bag as Feller pitched to Holmes. Holmes, given a second chance to drive in Masi, responded with a clean single, only the second hit off of Feller in the game. Masi scored the critical run to give Boston a 1–0 lead. Alvin Dark grounded out to end the inning, but Boston held the lead.

The Indians, especially Boudreau and Feller, thought they had been robbed. But they couldn't transfer their frustration to offense in the top of the ninth. Cleveland failed to score off Sain, and Boston took Game One by a 1–0 score on what many believed was a tainted run.

One newspaper columnist echoed Cleveland's thoughts. "The game was not without its arguments," the writer noted, "and the disputed play at second base in the eighth inning will provide enough fuel to last all winter in the hot-stove league. Had NL umpire Bill Stewart caught the play the same way the camera is supposed to have seen it, the teams might still be battling." Boudreau, carefully wording his thoughts to avoid being fined by the commissioner's office, was quoted in an Associated Press story as saying, "I thought I had him [Masi]. I tagged him on the shoulder. But that's just my opinion. Stewart had his. It isn't a complaint."

Cleveland did not let Game One's controversial play affect them for too long. The Indians won Game Two 4–1 the next day and Game Three 2–0. Game Four also went Cleveland's way by a 2–1 score. Feller was Cleveland's starter in Game Five, but he was knocked out in the top of the seventh as Boston scored six runs. The Braves won that game 11–5. Cleveland took Game Six in Boston 4–3 to win the Series, and Feller had the dubious distinction of being credited with both of the Indians' losses. Feller never pitched another inning in World Series competition.

Despite the joy of Cleveland winning its first World Series title in 28 years, many Indian fans were frustrated that Feller, who was destined for the Hall of Fame, had been denied a win by Stewart's call. This was the era when films of the World Series were shown in movie theaters. The days of instant replay and in-depth television coverage were still in the future. Many fans flocked to their local cinemas to see for themselves if Stewart had blown the call. Slow-motion photography confirmed what everyone but Stewart thought was obvious: Masi was out—out by a mile.

Chapter 13

The Imperfect Game: Harvey Haddix Is Denied Immortality (1959)

Baseball, like no other sport, has the capacity to elevate obscure players, if only for a moment, into the limelight. Players who were known only to those who religiously study the morning box scores, can, through the magic of the sport, gain overnight fame simply by their actions in a single game, inning, or at-bat. Perhaps the best example of this phenomenon is Don Larsen. His career pitching totals are not the stuff of which legends are made. In a 14-year career, Larsen won just 81 games and lost 91. During the 1954 season, Larsen probably wondered if he belonged in the major leagues at all, compiling a miserable 3–21 record as a starter for the Baltimore Orioles. Nevertheless, Larsen is now a much-sought-after baseball personality. He has dozens of requests every year to appear at banquets, card shows, and memorabilia auctions. Why? It's simple. For one afternoon, Don Larsen was the best pitcher on earth. On October 8, 1956, he faced 27 Brooklyn Dodger batters in Game Five of the World Series, and not one reached first base. He threw a perfect game, and in the World Series no less. Nobody before or since—not Mathewson, not Johnson, not Koufax, not Gibson—has equalled this feat. Not long ago Larsen was asked if he ever gets tired of discussing that one game of nearly four decades ago. Larsen simply replied, "No, why should I?"

While Larsen's feat took him in the neighborhood of two hours to complete, other players can gain everlasting fame in a matter of seconds. Al Gionfriddo robbed Joe DiMaggio of a home run with a spectacular running catch in Game Six of the 1947 World Series on a play which probably lasted no more than ten seconds. Yet the unheralded Gionfriddo (who vanished from the majors after 1947) was still receiving autograph requests in the mail well into the 1980s, many of them from fans who weren't even born in 1947. In 1992, Mickey Morandini of the Philadelphia Phillies achieved a degree of celebrity status by making an unassisted triple play in a late-season game in Pittsburgh. Immediately, Morandini's name became associated with a tremendous baseball achievement, and became part of the sport's lore. Perhaps someday the name Morandini will become synonymous with the idea of an unassisted triple play, just as the name Harvey Haddix has become forever linked with the idea of pitching perfection, albeit tainted pitching perfection.

Harvey "The Kitten" Haddix was born in Medway, Ohio, on September 18, 1925. Despite being a good lefthanded pitcher, a commodity always in demand in the major leagues, Haddix began his baseball career at a time when the minor leagues were blossoming and the road to the big leagues was a long one. Haddix persevered, however, and finally got his chance to perform in "the show" in 1952, when he was approaching his twenty-seventh birthday. As a member of the St. Louis Cardinals, Haddix went 2–2 in seven appearances in his rookie season. The next season, 1953, was clearly the best of what would be a fourteen-year career. Haddix recorded 20 victories against just nine losses. In his last outstanding campaign, 1954, Haddix was 18–13. By 1956, the Cardinals figured "The Kitten" had seen better days, and shipped him off to the Philadelphia Phillies in a mid-season trade involving four anonymous players. By 1958, Haddix was a member of the Cincinnati Reds' pitching staff where his mediocre 8–7 record made him expendable one more time, and at season's end he was shipped off to Pittsburgh.

Haddix remained a member of the Pirates' pitching staff until he was traded to Baltimore in 1963. Two lackluster seasons as an

Oriole reliever ended his days as a major-league hurler. Haddix was never known as a dominant pitcher, as his career record of 136–113 will attest. The Milwaukee Braves no doubt had trouble believing that Haddix was just an average pitcher, though, after one remarkable outing Haddix had against them on a May evening in County Stadium back in 1959.

The Milwaukee Braves had every reason to be optimistic going into the 1959 season. It had been seven years since the Braves' management had shocked the baseball establishment by pulling the team out of Boston, where it had resided since the birth of the National League in 1876, and transplanting it to Milwaukee, a city which had endured half a century without big-league baseball. The move proved to be a financial bonanza as attendance dramatically improved for the club. More important, the fortunes of the Braves also increased significantly on the field, and the inept Boston-based club was transformed into an immediate pennant contender in the brewery city. Milwaukee had captured back-to-back National League championships in 1957 and 1958 under the managerial guidance of Fred Haney, and laid claim to the title "world champions" when they squeaked by the powerful New York Yankees in the 1957 World Series. The Braves probably should have won the 1958 World Series as well, but lost to Casey Stengel's Yankees in seven games after winning three of the first four.

The Pittsburgh Pirates, meanwhile, were forming the nucleus of a team to be reckoned with. After finishing in a tie for last place with the Chicago Cubs in 1957, the Pirates emerged as serious contenders for the pennant the next year. With manager Danny Murtaugh instilling confidence into a club that was accustomed to losing (1927 had been the last pennant-winning season in Pittsburgh), the Pirates finished a very respectable second in 1958, but eight full games behind the Braves. The Pirates-Braves game on May 26, 1959, although relatively early in the season, would showcase two of the league's best teams. Some writers thought that it would be a preview of an excellent late-season pennant chase. No one could have anticipated that little Harvey Haddix would mesmerize County Stadium and trigger a philosophical debate over what exactly constitutes a perfect game.

There are games when a pitcher knows he is in a groove. On May 26, 1959, Harvey Haddix realized this was one of those nights for him. Everything was working. From the very first inning, when three Milwaukee Braves came up and all three went back to their dugout in quick succession, it was apparent that Haddix was on top of his game. After six innings had passed, and still no Brave had reached first base, there was little doubt that those who had the privilege of being ticketholders were witnessing something special. The phrases "no-hitter" and even "perfect game" were being whispered among the crowd. By the seventh inning, the usually partisan Milwaukee crowd was beginning to shift allegiance. The fans were actually cheering each time Haddix retired another frustrated Braves batter to keep his slate clean. There was only one problem, though. The Pirates, despite numerous chances, had failed to provide Haddix with any offensive support. The score was still 0–0. Surely, the fans thought, Pittsburgh could score at least one run to back up Haddix's bid for immortality. Couldn't they?

To the eighth the game went. Pittsburgh couldn't muster a run off Milwaukee's Lew Burdette. In the home half of the eighth, Milwaukee batters number 22, 23, and 24 all failed to reach base. Haddix was still perfect, but Pittsburgh's impotent offense was not helping. Perhaps impotent is the wrong word. By the time the game was over, the Pirates had recorded 12 hits off of Burdette, but the crafty veteran, who had defeated the mighty Yankees three times in the 1957 World Series, was still managing to keep Pittsburgh from scoring an all-important run.

In the ninth inning, Pittsburgh once again failed to generate enough offense to break the tie. Burdette was fashioning a shutout of his own, but it was a struggle and it was not pretty. In the bottom of the ninth, with the hometown Milwaukee crowd now solidly behind the diminutive Pirate southpaw, Haddix mowed down the Braves in order for the ninth time. Now 27 batters had failed to reach first base. What should have been a time of wild celebration for Haddix and the Pirates was turning into an extremely frustrating evening. The spectators at County Stadium greeted the final out in the ninth inning with a tremendous ovation. As far as they were concerned, Haddix had done his job. He was perfect through nine innings, a standard game. But there was nothing standard about this night in Milwaukee.

Before that night, there had been a grand total of six perfect games pitched in the history of major-league baseball, not including Larsen's gem in the 1956 World Series. And one of those six was dubious. John Richmond, of Worcester's National League club, had achieved the feat on June 12, 1880. John Ward, of Providence, did the same thing five days later. Nearly 79 years had passed and no National League pitcher had equalled the accomplishment of Richmond and Ward. Four American League hurlers, including Cy Young, had managed to not allow a single opponent to reach first base in a game, but no one in that league had recorded a similar whitewash since Chicago's Charlie Robertson in 1922. (The questionable perfect game was recorded by Boston's Ernie Shore in a 1917 game against Washington. Boston's starter, Babe Ruth, walked leadoff hitter Ray Morgan and was ejected from the game after striking the plate umpire to protest ball four. Shore relieved Ruth. Morgan was caught stealing, and Shore retired the next 26 Washington hitters. For years Shore was credited with pitching a perfect game, despite the fact that he did not start the game, and a runner had reached first base!) Clearly, the major leagues were overdue for a perfect game, but fate was to be cruel to Harvey Haddix this night.

With every reason to be dejected, Haddix trudged out to the mound to pitch in the bottom of the tenth inning. Pittsburgh had once again failed to score, but Haddix refused to give in. Three more Braves went down in succession. The same scenario unfolded in the eleventh. No Pirate scored, no Brave reached first base. Amazingly, after 12 innings, the score was still 0–0, and Haddix was still perfect. By this time Haddix had established a major league record of retiring 36 consecutive batters, breaking the old mark of 33 set by Brooklyn's Sam Kimber back in 1884, when pitchers were permitted to throw from a running start. Kimber's perfect game, a 0–0 tie with Toledo, was called because of darkness. Haddix was pitching in the era of night baseball and there was no possibility of darkness getting him off the hook.

On to inning 13. Pittsburgh once again could not post any

number other than zero in the runs column. Milwaukee came to bat. Their leadoff hitter was Felix Mantilla, a light-hitting Puerto Rican who was better known for his glove than his bat. Mantilla hit a ground ball to Pirates third baseman Don Hoak. To the dismay of the crowd, Hoak committed an error. Mantilla was safe at first. The perfect game was gone, but the no-hitter and shutout were still intact. Eddie Mathews, arguably the Braves' best all-around player, laid down a sacrifice bunt. Mathews was thrown out at first, but Mantilla was now stationed at second base with one out. Next up was powerful Hank Aaron, six years into his Hall of Fame career, and already recognized as a threat to knock one over the fence at any given moment. Murtaugh signalled Haddix to intentionally walk Aaron. There were now runners at second and first with one out. Joe Adcock, the Milwaukee first baseman, came to the plate.

Adcock, a tall, muscular slugger from Louisiana, finally broke Haddix's spell by blasting a home run over the right-centerfield wall. It was a weird scene. The hometown fans collectively groaned, even though their team had just won an extra-inning thriller. But controversy was still in the air. First, what was the final score? Mantilla touched third and home, but Aaron caused a scorekeeping headache by leaving the diamond after touching second base. Adcock was ruled out for "passing" Aaron. Aaron returned to the basepath to touch third and home, and the umpires originally recorded the game as a 2–0 Milwaukee win. However, the verdict was changed by the statisticians at the National League office, who pointed out that the only time more than one run can score on a game-ending hit is when the hit is an outside-the-park home run. Since Adcock had only been credited with a double, because of Aaron's baserunning error, the final score had to be changed to 1–0.

More important, was Haddix's effort a perfect game? Many baseball writers claimed it was. After all, he retired the first 27 men to face him, just as Young and Larsen had. Heck, he had done more than Ernie Shore, and historians considered Shore's 1917 game as perfect. But the major-league record keepers were adamant: Haddix had not been perfect. He had allowed a hit and three baserunners, even though all had reached base in the fateful thirteenth inning. As a consolation, Haddix's name appeared under "special mention" in the baseball record books for tossing 12 perfect innings. In the spring of 1992, it became official. According to a revised definition of no-hitters and perfect games passed by the major leagues, Haddix *did not* throw a perfect game on May 26, 1959. The new requirements stated a pitcher must not allow a hit in the entire game. "I knew it wasn't a no-hitter," Haddix, quoted in an Associated Press news story, said in 1992, thinking back to the night 33 years earlier when, for a few hours, he was the best pitcher on earth.

Chapter 14

Maris, Ruth, Frick, and the Asterisk: The Disputed Home-Run Record (1961)

> The monument had been erected thirty-four years before, in 1927, and was known as Babe Ruth's 60 Home Runs. Like "56" and ".406," that "60" was one of baseball's touchstone numbers, and suddenly it was under assault.
>
> —Donald Honig, in *Baseball America*, discussing Roger Maris' attempt to break one of the sport's most sacred records

> Check the history books. You'll see that [1961] was when the world began to go to hell, right after a .260 hitter broke Ruth's record.
>
> —A disgruntled Babe Ruth fan, quoted by Donald Honig in *Baseball America*

Baseball purists—and there are thousands of them—were a contented lot for 50 years. Beginning in 1903 and continuing through the 1952 season, major league baseball was a model of stability. The same 16 major league clubs operated every summer in the same cities, eight in the National League and eight in the American League. When the 1953 season began, traditionalists mourned a loss. It was the death of the Boston Braves, who, after drawing fewer than 300,000 paying spectators to their home games in 1952, did the unheard-of and moved their operations to Milwaukee. Financially, it was a great move for the Braves organization. Attendance figures multiplied by five. Still, to the purist, it was a sad thing to see the Boston Braves reduced to a memory. After all, the club had been representing the city of Boston in the National League since the circuit was founded in 1876. But sentiment did not pay the bills, and one of baseball's links to the past had been severed.

The success of the Braves' transfer to greener pastures made a few more owners reevaluate their priorities. The lowly St. Louis Browns, the longtime laughingstocks of the American League, left St. Louis after the 1953 season and set up shop in Baltimore as the Orioles. The Philadelphia Athletics, Connie Mack's baby, after years of fluctuating between greatness and ineptness, decided that Philadelphians had not been kind to them and moved to Kansas City in 1955. The baseball landscape was changing—too quickly for those who relished the sport's glorious past. The most shocking of the franchise shifts occurred after the 1957 season, when the New York Giants and Brooklyn Dodgers packed up their belongings, abandoned their antiquated stadiums, and settled in San Francisco and Los Angeles, respectively. It was one thing for the pitiful Boston Braves to leave town, but when the two most successful franchises in National League history abruptly ended their relationships with the Polo Grounds and Ebbets Field, something insidious seemed to be happening. Baseball would never be the same, and the purists bemoaned the losses with curses, tears, and anger.

The 1960 season would mark the end of an era in another respect which bothered traditionalists. The American League announced it was expanding from eight to ten teams beginning with the 1961 season. In a strange maneuver, the Washington Senators would move to Minneapolis and become the Minnesota Twins, while a new franchise would replace the Washington club in the District of Columbia and retain the name Senators. A new California-based entry, the Los Angeles Angels (later called California), would enter the circuit to complete the ten-team league. Few fans took note of it at the time, but the American League also announced that each team would play 162 games in 1961, an increase of eight games from the traditional 154 that had been part of the major league scene since the Taft administration.

The addition of eight more games to each club's schedule was a simple matter of mathematics as far as the American League was concerned. Under the old eight-team, 154-game format, each club played every other team 22 times during the regular season, 11 times at home and 11 times on the road. With two new teams entering the league, AL officials realized that some fundamental changes would have to take place. In order to retain a balanced schedule (each team playing the others the same number of times) the AL opted to have each club play the other nine teams 18 times each, nine times at home and nine times on the road. Nine times 18 equals 162. With these figures, the schedule stayed balanced and was only slightly longer than in the past. What possible difference could eight more games on a club's schedule make?

For Roger Maris of the New York Yankees, baseball commissioner Ford Frick, and the multitudes who cared about the sport's treasured records, eight additional games turned out to be highly significant. Undoubtedly, nobody who conceived of the expanded schedule even thought about the ramifications of a player challenging a seasonal record set in the days of 154 games. Anyway, those records, for the most part, had stood the test of time. Was anybody really going to threaten George Sisler's mark of 257 hits, set in 1920? Earl Webb's record for doubles in a season (67 in 1931) was also beyond reach, even with the extra games. And surely, Babe Ruth's fantastic accomplishment of 60 home runs in the 1927 season was absolutely secure. Wasn't it?

Ruth's record was seemingly as solid as the Rock of Gibraltar. It must have seemed unbelievable to the mere mortals who played major-league baseball in the 1920s. At that time, home runs were much less common than they are today, largely because the ball was not as tightly packed with yarn and cork as the ones used in modern games. In order to fully appreciate what Ruth did in 1927, it is necessary to examine the home-run statistics for the entire American League that season. Ruth, of course, led the league with 60 home runs. His teammate Lou Gehrig finished second with 47. Another

Yankee, Tony Lazzeri, was third, with just 18. As a team, the powerful New York Yankees of 1927 smashed 158 home runs. The Philadelphia Athletics had the second-highest team total, with only 56 homers! In other words, Babe Ruth hit more home runs in 1927 than any of the other seven AL teams did! This might be the most astonishing record in all of sports. Don't get the idea that Ruth was just hitting home runs or striking out. Ruth was making contact regularly. His 1927 batting average was .356.

Even as the ball became livelier during the 1930s, and home runs began clearing the fences at an alarming rate, Ruth's record stood unbroken. Hack Wilson had come close, and so had Hank Greenberg, but Ruth remained the king. By the mid–1950s, with Ruth dead, some optimistic Yankee followers suggested that Ruth's record might actually be challenged—not by Roger Maris (who the hell was Roger Maris?) but by Mickey Mantle, who had followed in the footsteps of Ruth, Gehrig, and DiMaggio as the focal point of the Bronx's baseball fans.

If anyone was even remotely capable of hitting 60 home runs in a season again, it was Mickey Mantle. A switch-hitter, Mantle blasted balls from both sides of the plate with equal authority. His clouts had the majesty of some of Ruth's. Many baseball writers, some of them holdovers from the Ruth years, claimed that Mantle's spectacular 565-foot home run at Washington's Griffith Stadium in 1953 was the longest home run ever hit by anybody anywhere. Mantle was a proven commodity, having hit 37 home runs in 1955, 52 in 1956, 42 in 1958, and 40 in 1960. Surely, if anyone had a chance to break the great Babe's record, it was Mantle.

Roger Maris, on the other hand, was a virtual unknown when he first donned the Yankee pinstripes in 1960. His first big-league experience came in 1957, when he played in 116 games as an outfielder for Cleveland. Partway through the 1958 season, Maris was traded to the Kansas City A's, where he stayed through the 1959 season. In 1959, Maris hit 16 home runs. When he arrived in New York in 1960—Casey Stengel's last season as the Yankees' manager—Maris, a lefthanded hitter, found Yankee Stadium's short right-field fence to his liking, and hit 39 home runs. Not bad, but certainly not comparable to Mantle or Ruth.

When the 1961 season began, there was absolutely no indication that Maris would even begin to hit home runs at a terrific rate. It took 11 games for the first one to come, on April 26. At the end of May, Maris had 12 homers. But by the end of June, Maris' home run total had reached 27, two more than Ruth had hit by that point in 1927. Still, few thought that Maris had a legitimate chance. After all, Ruth's most productive month had been September, when he hit 17. Furthermore, Mantle was matching Maris home run for home run, and Mantle was getting the lion's share of publicity. This actually pleased Maris, who was uncomfortable being scrutinized by New York's relentless media.

July 25, 1961, was the real turning point for Maris, the day he began to believe he truly had a chance to make a run at Ruth. That evening, in a home doubleheader against the White Sox, Maris hit four home runs to up his total to 40. Ruth hadn't reached 40 until August 22. Now the media were beginning to badger Maris. Dozens of times a day Maris faced the question, "Can you break Ruth's record?" As the pressure began to mount, his answers became more abrupt and callous. The situation began to affect Maris' health. His hair began to fall out in clumps and his appetite waned. Some nights he didn't get any sleep. But still his bat was producing home runs. The fiftieth one came on August 22 in Los Angeles. By September 9 he had reached 56.

When it became apparent that Maris actually could surpass the Babe, questions about the expanded schedule suddenly entered the picture. Shouldn't Maris be judged on how many he had hit after 154 games? Who knows how many more Ruth may have hit if he had played another eight games? The length of the schedule became a preoccupation for sportswriters across the country. How much of an advantage was Maris getting by playing a 162-game schedule?

Other factors were also being discussed. Ruth was hitting a "dead ball," argued the traditionalists. Maris, replied the modernists, was contending with jet lag. Ruth played all of his games in the blistering heat of day games, while Maris had the luxury of playing at night. Ruth was facing pitchers who could legally throw trick pitches such as the spitball. Maris was facing black as well as white pitchers; Ruth played in an all-white league. Expansion had diluted the talent pool. Athletes were better conditioned in 1961 than in 1927. On and on it went, point followed by counterpoint. It made for great debate and generated tremendous excitement, but still no one was quite certain how major league baseball would handle the situation if Maris happened to overtake Ruth in the final eight games. Then Commissioner Ford Frick stepped in. Frick, a former New York sportswriter who had been friendly with Ruth, announced that Maris would have to hit 61 home runs in the first 154 games to legitimately break Ruth's record. If he hit his sixty-first homer afterward, it would be listed in the record book with an asterisk and a notation stating that the record was set in an expanded schedule. Of course, this added even more fuel to the burning debate.

Maris became angry at the entire issue. Now not only did he have to hit 61 home runs, he had to do it within a given time frame. "Which 154 games am I supposed to do it in?" Maris asked sarcastically. "The first 154? The last 154? Or the 154 in the middle of the schedule?" As the debate rolled on, so did Maris. On September 17, he hit home run number 58 in the Yankees' 152nd game of the season. On September 20, in Baltimore, the Yankees played their 154th game of the season (actually it was the 155th; a tie game early in the season had clouded the issue even further). That night, according to Frick's edict, was the last chance Maris had to eclipse the Babe. He hit a home run in the third inning off of Milt Pappas. It was number 59. He went homerless in the remainder of the game. Despite the homer, one New York newspaper's headline read "Maris Fails."

There were about two weeks left in the season. Maris hit number 60 on September 26 at Yankee Stadium. On the final day of the season, October 1, Maris hit his sixty-first home run of the 1961 campaign, off Boston's Tracy Stallard. It landed in Yankee Stadium's lower-deck seats in right field and was retrieved by 19-year-old Sal Durante, who presented Maris with the ball after the game in the Yankee clubhouse.

So who was the real home-run champion now? It was not an easy matter to decide. Maris had played in 161 of his team's games. Ruth, in 1927, had appeared in 150. Maris had a home run taken away when a rainout had prevented five innings from being played. Ruth had had no such misfortune. Maris had 590 at-bats in 1961, compared to Ruth's 540. Maris had the luxury of having Mickey Mantle (who ended up with 54 homers) bat behind him in the Yankee lineup; he was not given an intentional walk all season. Babe Ruth, with Lou Gehrig batting after him, had had a similar advantage.

When the record books were printed after the season, Babe Ruth was listed as having hit 60 home runs in a 154-game schedule. Right after Ruth's name was Roger Maris, whose 61 homers were noted as having been accomplished in a 162-game schedule. There was no asterisk separating the two men, but the notation about the length of their respective schedules had the same effect.

As late as 1987, a national sports talk show asked viewers to call a toll-free number to vote on who should be considered the true home-run champion. An overwhelming majority, 89 percent, favored Maris, who had died of cancer in 1985 at the age of 51, still unable to shake the ghost of Ruth. Perhaps the whole argument was best summed up by baseball historian Donald Honig in his outstanding book *Baseball America*:

> Many people supported Frick, while others contended that a season was a season, which sounds reasonable but really isn't, for if the season had been extended to 175 games they would have been singing not just a different tune but different lyrics.

Chapter 15

The Speed Game: Was Lou Brock Out at Home? (1968 World Series)

> There's no secret about Lou Brock; he's fast. Give him credit.
>
> —St. Louis catcher Tim McCarver, on Brock's base-stealing ability

If Lou Brock was not the most gifted baserunner ever to play major league baseball, there are very few ahead of him on the list. Brock, along with Maury Wills of the Los Angeles Dodgers, reintroduced the concept of foot speed to baseball. In the process, they caused their opponents to have fits.

At the start of the twentieth century, baseball had been a game of advancing the runner one base at a time. With the ball lacking the spring it would later have, long home runs and power hitters were very scarce commodities. Runs were scored with sacrifice bunts, hit-and-run plays, and stolen bases. Ty Cobb and Eddie Collins were masters of this type of play, both having the raw speed and bat control to play what Giants manager John McGraw referred to as "inside baseball." During the 1920s and especially the 1930s, with the introduction of the live ball, the immediacy of the home run caused a radical change in the way baseball was played. Clever baserunning became outdated and largely a novelty. Jimmie Foxx, Hank Greenberg, and others who possessed thunderous bats became the rage. Stolen bases became almost as rare as home runs had once been.

By the 1947 season stolen bases, especially in the American League, were becoming obsolete. Bob Dillinger of the St. Louis Browns led the AL in stolen bases in 1947 with 34. The following year he topped the league again, this time with 28. When Dillinger won his third straight stolen-base championship in 1949, the scant total of 20 was sufficient. Dominic DiMaggio of the Red Sox ended Dillinger's reign atop the AL stolen-base plateau in 1950, but his tiny total of 15 did not exactly make it a highly coveted title. At this steadily declining rate, some feared the stolen base might be going the way of the dodo bird.

Stolen-base totals in the twenties and thirties were usually enough to lead either major league through the 1950s. Then Maury Wills came along. Beginning with his 50 steals in 1960, Wills demonstrated that speed could kill. From 1960 through 1965, Wills won six straight NL stolen-base crowns. In 1962 he stole an unheard-of 104 bases to erase Ty Cobb's old major league mark of 96, which had stood since 1915. Wills' thefts weren't just for show; the Dodgers needed every one of them. Gone were the days when Dodger teams had pounded their opponents into submission with home runs. Tight, low-scoring pitching duels were becoming the norm, and every base Wills pilfered was greatly appreciated by the Los Angeles pitching staff, who needed as much offensive support as the speedy Wills could provide.

Lou Brock continued where Wills left off. Acquired in 1964 by the St. Louis Cardinals from the Chicago Cubs in one of baseball's most one-sided trades, Brock immediately showed the form which one day would allow him to eclipse Ty Cobb's all-time stolen base record. In the nine seasons from 1966 to 1974 Brock led the NL eight times in stolen bases. The year of his final stolen base title, 1974, Brock, at the age of 35, shattered Wills' old major league standard by swiping 118 bases. Brock, a native of Arkansas, stole 938 career bases by the time he hung up his spikes after the 1979 season.

Brock appeared in three World Series with the Cardinals. In his first World Series, in 1964, Brock somehow did not steal a base in the seven games against the New York Yankees. In 1967, St. Louis' next World Series appearance, Brock made up for his unimpressive showing in 1964 by stealing seven bases against the Boston Red Sox and estabishing a World Series record. In the 1968 World Series Brock duplicated his feat of the previous autumn, stealing another seven against the Detroit Tigers. Brock's 14 career steals in World Series play rank him number one in history.

Despite this record, Brock is largely remembered for another baserunning incident in the World Series, one which had nothing to do with a stolen-base attempt. With St. Louis just one win away from eliminating the Tigers in the 1968 Series, Brock tried to score from second base on a single. Brock crossed home plate without attempting to slide, and was tagged out by Tigers catcher Bill Freehan in a play which completely shifted the momentum of the World Series. Some agree with plate umpire Doug Harvey's call. Others maintain that Brock should have been called safe. Virtually everybody agrees that Brock would have been safe if he had opted to slide.

The idea that a baserunning error would decide the 1968 World Series should have been ridiculous. Pitchers had dominated the 1968 season as they had no other. Denny McLain, Detroit's free-spirited right-hander, had won 31 games. Nobody since Dizzy Dean in 1934 had managed a 30-win season, but McLain, pitching on three days' rest, made it look easy. Detroit manager Mayo Smith was so enamored of McLain that he allowed his star hurler a few extra liberties on his off days. One of those perks was that McLain was allowed to play the organ professionally and promote his musical career. It wasn't at all unusual for the 24-year-old McLain to make several cross-country plane trips in the space of a week, shuttling between organ gigs and American League ballparks. With McLain leading the way, Detroit romped to the AL flag, 12 full games ahead of second-place Baltimore.

Matching McLain for skill in the National League was Bob Gibson, who could never be confused with the outgoing McLain in personality. Gibson, everyone's choice for the surliest man in the majors, was the ace of the Cardinals' pitching staff. Gibson's record in 1968 was a very good 22–9, but that didn't tell half the story. What everybody was talking about was Gibson's amazing 1.12 earned run average. Years later, Don Drysdale of the Dodgers said Gibson's ERA was "almost obscene." Not once in Gibson's 34 starts did Cardinals manager Red Schoendienst have to replace him on the mound. A menacing figure, the 6′1″ Gibson recorded 13 shutouts and whiffed 268 opposing batters. With Game One of the World Series set for Busch Stadium, baseball fans were almost drooling about the pitching matchup for the opener: McLain versus Gibson.

Fans of Bob Gibson relished Game One. Gibson, displaying the tools which had crushed the wills of NL batters all season, struck out 17 Tigers, setting a World Series record. McLain, who lasted only until the sixth inning, called Gibson's performance "the single greatest pitching feat I ever saw." Assisted by a Lou Brock home run, the Cards won easily, 4–0. The next afternoon, Detroit's Mickey Lolich was the pitching hero, going the distance for an 8–1 victory. Lolich even hit his first (and last) major league home run in the game to cap the win.

When the series shifted to Detroit for the next three contests, the Cardinals seemed to enjoy Tiger Stadium more than the home team did. Tim McCarver's three-run homer in the fifth inning of Game Three sparked St. Louis to a 7–3 win. Gibson was his usual brilliant self in Game Four, pitching his normal nine stellar innings in St. Louis' 10–1 romp. McLain lost again, this time lasting just two and two-thirds innings. St. Louis was now just one win away from repeating as World Series champions.

Game Five, the final game at Tiger Stadium in 1968, featured two controversial incidents. The first one was trivial, having nothing to do with the game itself. It revolved around the performance of the national anthem by popular folk singer José Feliciano. Instead of warbling the "Star Spangled Banner" in the traditional manner, Feliciano's rendition, according to *The New York Times*, was "similar to a blend between soul and folksinging styles." Whatever it was, it drew a decidedly mixed reaction from the crowd, many booing throughout the rendition. NBC's Tony Kubek said Feliciano "did a heck of a job." Tiger radio announcer Ernie Harwell, who had recommended Feliciano in the first place, agreed. Others weren't so complimentary. Joe Oyler, brother of Tigers shortstop Ray Oyler, told reporters, "I'm young enough to understand it, but I think it stunk." One irate female fan declared she would "write to my senator about it."

While Feliciano had the nation momentarily abuzz, a more substantial and enduring controversy occurred in the fifth inning. St. Louis opened up a three-run lead in the top of the first inning, courtesy of Orlando Cepeda's three-run homer. Detroit, now fighting for their lives, struck back for two runs in the home half of the fourth inning to narrow the Cardinals' advantage to 3–2. With one out in the top of the fifth, Lou Brock got his third hit of the game, a double. Next up was Cardinals second baseman Julian Javier. He laced a hit off of Mickey Lolich which landed in left field in front of Tigers outfielder Willie Horton. Brock, who had left second with the crack of the bat, rounded third and charged toward the plate. Horton fielded the ball cleanly and unleashed a perfect throw toward catcher Bill Freehan. With the ball on its way, Freehan, within the bounds of the rules, placed his left foot in front of the plate, taking away a few precious inches from Brock. Brock, noticing Freehan's foot, elected not to slide, but rather opted to try to score standing up. Television replays indicate Brock's speed took him to the *general area* of the plate before Horton's throw hit Freehan's glove. As Brock was passing the Detroit catcher, Freehan wheeled around and appeared to tag him. Plate umpire Doug Harvey, positioned perfectly to make the call, immediately ruled Brock out.

Within seconds, Brock, manager Schoendienst, and on-deck hitter Curt Flood descended upon Harvey to challenge what they figured was an obviously bad call. While Harvey conceded that Brock had beaten Horton's throw, he had called Brock out as soon as Freehan applied the tag because, in his opinion, Brock had not touched the plate. The arguing, of course, did not sway Harvey, a seven-year veteran NL umpire. The Cardinal rally died, which proved to be costly. Detroit tallied three runs in the seventh inning (the key blow being Al Kaline's bases-loaded single) and won the game 5–3.

As for the play at the plate, Brock was quoted in *The New York Times* afterward: "In my opinion, it was the biggest play of the game. We had the makings of a big inning, and instead of one run, one man on and one out, there were two outs and no runs." In the Cardinals' dugout, the players watched with keen interest the NBC monitor, which was showing replays of Brock trying to score. According to the partisan view of the Cardinals, they had been robbed.

"I had it beat; I beat the ball to the plate," claimed Brock. "There was no doubt about it. It wasn't even close. He [Harvey] didn't call me out because it was close. He called me out for not touching the plate. I touched the middle of the plate." As an afterthought, Brock added, "I didn't slide because I didn't think I had to."

The other notable player in this controversy, catcher Bill Freehan, had a drastically different opinion on what happened. "I think I had the worst view in America. I was looking for the throw and reaching for the ball. I expected [Brock] to slide, and when he didn't, his foot left spike marks in the dirt about half an inch from the plate." Commenting on Brock's odd decision not to slide, Freehan said, "I think he would have been safe if he had slid. Later the umpire told me the same thing."

Because of the position of the television cameras and the careful placement of Freehan's foot, it is difficult to determine whether or not Brock actually touched the plate. Certainly, he did not touch the middle of it, as he claimed. Still photos provided by the Associated Press seem to back up Freehan's assertion that Brock's foot landed short of the plate. Detroit, now down only three games to two, traveled to St. Louis feeling that Brock's decision not to slide had given them another life. On only two days' rest, McLain pitched Game Six for Detroit. Finally, he had a dominant outing. The Tigers tied a World Series record by scoring ten runs in the third inning, more than enough to coast to a 13–1 win. In Game Seven, Gibson, trying to win his third game of the Series, proved he was fallible after all. The Tigers broke open a scoreless tie in the seventh inning with three runs. Both teams scored once in the ninth, but it was too little for St. Louis. Mickey Lolich had his third win of the Series, and Detroit had rallied to win the 1968 World Series in seven games after trailing three games to one. Clearly, the momentum of the World Series dramatically shifted from St. Louis to Detroit after

Brock was declared out at home. If Brock had slid and was safe, St. Louis would have led Game Five 4–2 and have been in a good position to tack on at least one more run. Detroit may have been as good as dead if Brock had slid. Undoubtedly, Harvey's call constituted the biggest play of the 1968 World Series.

In the mid–1980s, long after all the participants of the 1968 World Series had left the major leagues (all except Doug Harvey, who retired only after the 1992 season), Mickey Lolich, the surprise pitching star of the Series, reminisced about the memorable seven games. He recalled the thrill of winning three of the games, his amazement at hitting his first big league homer in Game Two, the Tigers rallying to win the Series after being down three games to one, and of course, the disputed play at home plate in Game Five. When asked by a television reporter whether one moment stood out above all the rest as the most memorable of the whole 1968 World Series, Lolich grinned for a moment and replied, "That's easy. José Feliciano screwing up the national anthem!"

Chapter 16

Too Much Hustle? Pete Rose Flattens Ray Fosse (1970 All-Star Game)

Throughout his career, a career that should have led to a plaque in Cooperstown, Pete Rose played the game the only way he knew how—aggressively. With the competitive values instilled in him by his father, Rose, from the time he shattered a window with a line drive at age three in his family's yard to his final major league at-bat in 1986, asserted himself whenever he stepped onto the playing field. His major league career transcended three decades. It began at a time when a $15,000 salary was considered very good and ended when some big leaguers sulked when their yearly earnings were only near the $500,000 mark. Values had changed, baseball had changed, but Pete Rose had not. As far as Rose was concerned, each game was a battle. It could be savored as well played, but it must be played hard, whether it be a meaningless late-season game between pennant also-rans or the seventh game of the World Series. In his 24 years in the majors, no one could ever accuse Rose of not trying his hardest.

While some people reveled in Rose's hard-nosed philosophy of how the game ought to be played, others thought that his ultra-high level of competitiveness could sometimes drift beyond the bounds of common sense. Rose's impressive 1978 hitting streak is a good example. During the summer of 1978, Rose began collecting hits on a regular basis—so regular, in fact, that some wondered if he had a legitimate chance to challenge Joe DiMaggio's legendary 56-game hitting streak, a record which had stood majestically since 1941. As the number of consecutive games with hits continued to mount, so did the pressure and media attention. This intense scrutiny would have caused lesser individuals to crack or seek places of refuge. Not so with Rose. As his streak passed the 30- and 40-game marks, Rose seemed to relish the attention he was getting. He eagerly answered reporters' queries about his chances of surpassing the great DiMaggio in the record books. More than that, Pete Rose was having fun! He loved an athletic challenge, and DiMaggio's seemingly untouchable record was one perfectly suited to Rose's competitive spirit. It required day-by-day excellence with no margin for a bad game at the plate. When his streak finally ended—in Atlanta, after 44 games—those who expected Rose to heave a sigh of relief knew little about what made Rose tick. Asked by a reporter if the end of his challenge to DiMaggio's mark was a burden off his shoulders, Rose, amazed by what he thought was a silly question, replied, "No, I'm pissed off!"

That incident encapsulated Rose's fiery competitiveness. Others might have been satisfied with a 44-game hitting streak, but not Rose. He wanted the challenge to continue. There should always be goals to strive for. Complacency, according to Rose, was akin to laziness.

Pete Rose first stepped into the batter's box in a major league game as a member of the Cincinnati Reds in 1963. In his first plate appearance, he drew a base on balls. There was no such thing as a "walk" in Pete Rose's mind. He ran the 90 feet down to first base, and never stopped running until 1986, when he deemed his reflexes were no longer capable of producing the results which his inner drive demanded. From that first plate appearance in 1963 to his final one (a strikeout) in 1986, six different men had occupied the White House. Pete Rose, or "Charlie Hustle" as the media referred to him, was constant: Never giving an inch, always scrapping for that extra edge.

Images of Rose at work are varied. Some recall the head-first slides, the pumping fists, the balls slammed into the turf after third outs. Some remember the pure joy Rose felt in simply playing the game he loved. During the high tension of Game Six of the 1975 World Series, a contest which must be listed as one of the most nerve-racking in sports history, Rose, standing on third base, asked Boston's Rico Petrocelli, "Isn't this fun?" Petrocelli just stared at Rose in disbelief, refusing to accept that any rational human being could be enjoying such a nail-biting affair. And other fans choose to recall the emotional evening in Cincinnati's Riverfront Stadium when Pete Rose finally surpassed Ty Cobb with hit number 4,192. Rose ripped a single off of San Diego's Eric Show. The ball dropped onto the artificial turf in center field. Rose ran to first, made a big turn in case there was an opportunity to reach second base, and then retreated to the bag he had just rounded. He was greeted by his son, a Reds batboy, who embraced him. Both broke into tears, the enormity of the occasion overwhelming them. Rose, despite his intensity, was human after all.

There is one enduring image of Rose which is as much a part of the man as the 44-game hitting streak and the 4,256 career hits. It is a single baserunning incident, one that Rose admirers discuss with pride and those who object to Rose's recklessness recall with disgust and horror. Any baseball fan worth his or her salt has seen it at least once, and after seeing it, the image is burned into one's mind: Rose rounding third with the winning run. Catcher Ray Fosse blocking the plate. Rose blasting Fosse to the turf with all of his might. Rose is safe. The game is over—the 1970 All-Star Game! Pete Rose creamed a catcher in an All-Star Game, a game which doesn't count in the standings and has no bearing on individual statistics! Yet there was Rose, in all his competitive fury, mowing down poor Ray Fosse. You either loved it or hated it. No middle ground is possible.

All-star games, by nature, are passive things. They are glitzy events more than fiercely fought contests. Baseball was the first of the major sports to have a game played solely by the most outstanding individuals of the day. A Chicago sportswriter, Arch Ward, dreamed up the idea in the early 1930s, and the first major-league All-Star Game took place at old Comiskey Park in 1933. Babe Ruth homered to give the American League a 4–2 victory in that initial contest. Over the years, the annual All-Star Game began to take on a more serious tone. There had always been a genuine rivalry between National League and American League players, and the July game was one method of deciding which circuit was superior.

Eventually, all-star fever was incorporated into the other major sports. Football's version, the Pro Bowl, is probably the worst. It seems that every NFL player wants to be named to one of the teams, yet very few are actually interested in playing the game. No one wants to risk a serious injury, and special rules prohibit aggressive play. The end result is usually a yawn-inspiring, watered-down game which fails to generate any true enthusiasm. In recent years, the National Hockey League has also shown the world how bad all-star games can be. With an unwritten rule stating that body contact is forbidden, the defense takes a holiday. Offenses run amock and "pond-hockey scores," as Wayne Gretzky calls them, have become commonplace. Fans who enjoy tight-checking, well-played games have responded by turning their television sets off. Basketball's all-star game is only slightly better. The scores often reach the 150-point mark for each team, but nobody really seems to mind, since basketball is by nature a high-scoring sport.

Baseball, almost by default, has been left with the most meaningful of the all-star games. Except for the 1945 season, when wartime travel restrictions prevented it from being played, the contest has become a symbol of summer and a symbol of baseball itself. But still it is an exhibition game, one where new friends are made, interleague animosities are put aside for a few days, and a good time is supposed to be had by all. Sure, there is a game to be played and the honor of the two leagues is at stake, but nobody really expects the players to engage in a vicious battle. Apparently Pete Rose was not told about this. A game was a game to him, and he demonstrated this quite conclusively on July 14, 1970, in his home park, Cincinnati's Riverfront Stadium.

With President Richard Nixon among the sellout crowd, both teams took the field as NBC beamed the contest across North America. For the first time since 1957, the starting lineups had been elected by fan balloting. As in 1957, when obvious ballot-box stuffing had embarrassed baseball's hierarchy, there were some complaints that fans had voted with their hearts instead of their heads. Nevertheless, the array of talent on hand was impressive. The National League had won every All-Star Game since 1963, and were looking to make it eight straight. Starting for the NL was glamorous Tom Seaver of the defending World Series champion New York Mets. Taking the mound for the AL was Jim Palmer of the Baltimore Orioles. Both men pitched the maximum three innings allowed by the rules, and both did their jobs well. After three innings the score was 0–0.

The American League broke the deadlock in the sixth with one run and held a comfortable 4–1 lead going into the bottom of the ninth. With their winning streak in imminent danger, the National League fought back with three runs to tie the score at 4–4. The game went into extra innings, which suited the NL just fine: in the history of the major-league All-Star Game, the NL had won every game which had gone beyond the regulation nine innings. Nothing was decided in the tenth or eleventh innings. Claude Osteen of the Los Angeles Dodgers, the fifth NL pitcher of the evening, shut down the AL in the top of the twelfth inning. Clyde Wright of the California Angels, the AL's seventh hurler, would try to neutralize the NL hitters in the bottom of the inning.

The chance that the game would enter the thirteenth inning was becoming more and more likely as Wright disposed of the first two NL batters. Pete Rose, the next NL hitter, who had failed to connect in his previous turns at the plate, gave the NL some hope with a solid single. Bill Grabarkewitz of the Dodgers also singled, sending Rose to second. Into the batter's box stepped Jim Hickman of the Chicago Cubs. Hickman was lucky to be at the game at all, his airline connections having been messed up. With his travel troubles behind him, Hickman knocked a single into center field in front of outfielder Amos Otis. Rose, realizing he had the chance to end the game, had no intention of stopping at third base. The correspondent from UPI described the sight:

> Rose came around third like an express train, had the throw by center fielder Amos Otis beaten anyway, but charged into [Cleveland Indians' catcher Ray] Fosse and sent him sprawling to insure the tally.

Rose had scored, the NL had won an exciting contest 5–4 in 12 innings, but that was all secondary to those who watched the game end. The real story was Rose levelling Fosse, who had made the mistake of standing in front of home plate to receive Otis' throw. Rose must have seen that Fosse was not ready to tag him. Nevertheless, Rose blasted the 23-year-old backstop, who was making his first appearance in an All-Star Game. Rose became the premier story, overshadowing the game itself. One syndicated UPI report of the game began this way:

> Pete Rose, Cincinnati's hometown star, bowled catcher Ray Fosse over at home plate to score on Jim Hickman's single in the 12th inning last night to give the NL its eighth consecutive victory, 5–4, over the AL.

After the tremendous collision, both men were hurt. Fosse was on his knees, unable to rise. Rose asked him if he were badly injured. Fosse was. He had severely damaged his left shoulder. He would never be able to hit the ball with the same power he once had. The sheer force of Rose running into Fosse injured Pete's left knee. Rose would have to nurse his wound and miss Cincinnati's next three games. In the entire decade of the 1970s, Rose was sidelined for only ten games due to injury, and 30 percent of them were due to his collision with Ray Fosse. Fosse himself somehow managed to play in Cleveland's next game.

When asked about the play by reporters after the game, Rose said he was sorry he had to run into Fosse, but he "would have broken both legs" if he had slid. Fosse—who, by coincidence, had become friendly with Rose during the All-Star break and had been a guest at Rose's house—was convinced that Rose meant no harm. "I know he didn't mean to do it," said Fosse in a UPI story. "It all happened so quick. I never got hit like that before. Who knows? Maybe he should have run around me."

The play made Rose famous. It was shown time and time again to a national audience which knew little about Rose. After all, Rose played in the small market of Cincinnati. People would get to know more about Rose and the Reds. Cincinnati made five post-season appearances between 1970 and 1976, winning two World Series.

Years later, Roger Kahn, Rose's biographer (*Pete Rose: My Story*), spoke to both Rose and Fosse about the famous collision. Kahn asked Fosse why he had even bothered to block the plate. Why not just let Rose score? Fosse replied,

> That's the wrong play. The right play is to block the plate. I knew 65 million people were watching on TV. Aside from that, I wanted the respect of my peers. I wasn't going to look like a fool and get out of the way. I was the Cleveland catcher, not the San Diego chicken.

Rose, predictably, still had little remorse. "Look," he told Kahn. "I'm the winning run in the All-Star Game in my home town. I just want to get to that plate as quickly as I can." As an afterthought Rose added, "Besides, nobody told me they had changed it to girls' softball between third and home."

That was the way Pete Rose played baseball. He played it hard and he played it tough. No apologies were necessary. If he had played it any other way, he wouldn't have been Pete Rose.

Chapter 17

Blind Justice: Ken Burkhart's Behind-the-Back Call (1970 World Series)

Keep your eye everlastingly on the ball while it is in play.
—General Instructions to Umpires,
in *The Official Rules of Baseball*

Television and baseball have had a prosperous partnership for more than half a century. Beginning with a blurry picture of Brooklyn's Ebbets Field in 1939, the piercing eye of the television camera has brought millions of viewers the remarkable sights that are a part of baseball's rich history. The intensity and drama of the World Series has been personalized through the magic of television. Those old enough to remember the gripping afternoon of October 8, 1956, when New York's Don Larsen captivated a nation with a perfect game, can attest to the power of the medium which transmitted the event. When color broadcasts of sports became a reality, the emotions displayed between the lines became even more apparent. Bill Mazeroski's Series-winning homer in 1960, Carlton Fisk's famous body-English homer in 1975, and Kirk Gibson's improbable blast in 1988 were all magnified by the presence of television.

If television has one flaw, it is the fact that it shows exactly what is happening, be it a thing of majesty, like Ron Swoboda's unbelievable catch in the 1969 World Series, or a scene of ugliness, such as the behavior of the St. Louis Cardinals during the seventh game of the 1985 World Series. Television, in all its truthfulness, was on hand for Game One of the 1970 World Series, and objectively showed a nation of baseball fans how badly a play can be bungled. Three key characters played starring roles in this farce: Cincinnati's Bernie Carbo, who tried to score from third base on a batted ball which traveled only a few feet from home plate; Baltimore catcher Elrod Hendricks, who somehow did not see Carbo charging toward him; and umpire William "Ken" Burkhart, who was trampled by Hendricks, missed the phantom tag Hendricks applied to Carbo, and made one of the most comically inept calls ever. The entire play has, over time, become so infamous that it is used in umpiring instructional videos to demonstrate how *not* to make a call.

The 1970 season was only the second in baseball history to feature a tier of playoff games before the World Series. The League Championship Series, as they were officially called, came into being in 1969. That year, both major leagues expanded their membership to include two new franchises. The fledgling entries in the American League were the Kansas City Royals and the Seattle Pilots. (The Pilots would survive just one season in Seattle before relocating to Milwaukee as the Brewers.) The National League was more creative, placing clubs in San Diego and Montreal. The idea of a Canadian franchise in major-league baseball was appalling to some, including a group of U.S. senators who tried to prevent the Expos from playing in 1969. The four new teams brought the total of major-league franchises to 24, 12 in each league. Commissioner Bowie Kuhn felt that two loops of 12 clubs was cumbersome, and instituted a radical reform measure. Each league was divided into two divisions of six clubs. Instead of the traditional two pennant races, which had been in place since the turn of the century, there were now four. The divisional champions within each league would meet in a best-of-five series to determine an overall league titleholder to play in the World Series.

Traditionalists cringed at the whole concept. Baseball, they said, was becoming like basketball and hockey, bloating the number of clubs annually qualifying for postseason play. Teams could now advance to the World Series because of a lucky stretch of three games instead of on the basis of the tried-and-true, grueling full-season schedule. Purists were quick to point out that the 1969 New York Mets, winners of the World Series, had been the NL's laughingstocks in previous seasons. Never finishing higher than ninth in the old ten-team NL, the Mets had won the newly created National League East, had defeated Atlanta in the first NLCS, and had upset a heavily favored Baltimore Orioles club in the World Series. This was a travesty, the traditionalists moaned. This is the wave of the future, said the commissioner's office, and the League Championship Series was here to stay.

In 1970, fans were still getting accustomed to four separate pennant races. Geography teachers were having difficulty explaining to their baseball-loving students that although Atlanta was close to the Atlantic coast and Chicago was located in the middle of the country, the great minds of major-league baseball had placed Atlanta in the NL West and Chicago in the NL East. Almost forgotten in the discussion about realignment was the fact that two very solid baseball clubs were emerging from the rest: the Cincinnati Reds and the Baltimore Orioles. Under rookie manager George "Sparky" Anderson (who already had gray hair at age 36), the Reds rolled to an easy NL West crown in 1970, winning 102 games along the way. Baltimore's season was equally impressive: the Orioles won 108 games to make a mockery of the race in the AL East. The League Championship Series proved to be just a formality for both the Reds and the Orioles. Cincinnati crushed Pittsburgh in three straight games, while Baltimore administered the same punishment to the Minnesota Twins. The World Series was set to open in Cincinnati on the afternoon of October 10. Six umpires received the prestigious honor of being selected to work the 1970 World Series. Three of them—Emmett Ashford, John Flaherty, and Robert Stewart—were American League veterans. The other three were from the National League—William Williams, Anthony Venzon, and the soon-to-be-famous Ken Burkhart.

Game One was a milestone in World Series history. For the first time in the 67-year history of the event, a World Series game would be contested on artificial turf. Newly built Riverfront Stadium, which had replaced aging Crosley Field as the home of the Reds, featured the plastic grass, much to the dismay of the purists. Also dismayed were the Baltimore Orioles, whose only experience on the ersatz turf was when they played in Kansas City. Manager Earl Weaver, who was already considered the most hot-tempered pilot in the majors, was concerned that the fast carpet in Cincinnati's home park would disrupt the timing of his team. Series analysts foresaw the turf as a potentially key advantage for the Reds. All season long they had alternated between Riverfront Stadium and traditional National League parks with grass, and were used to the drastic difference. As it turned out, the playing surface played no real role in determining which club would emerge as world champions for 1970. A bizarre call by plate umpire Ken Burkhart in the sixth inning of Game One made quite a bit of difference, though.

The pitching matchup for the Series opener was intriguing. For the visiting Baltimore Orioles, Earl Weaver nominated Jim Palmer, a handsome right-hander, who had won 20 games for the Orioles in 1970. For Cincinnati, Sparky Anderson countered with Gary Nolan, just 22 years old but already pitching in his fourth major league season. Nolan had notched an 18–7 record in the regular season, and had defeated Pittsburgh in Game One of the NLCS seven days earlier. The Reds, playing in their first World Series since 1961, opened the scoring early with a run in the bottom of the first inning. A two-run homer by Reds first baseman Lee May in the third inning put Cincinnati up 3–0. The Orioles, however, were not in the mood for surrender, and began to use Earl Weaver's favorite weapon—the home run—to strike back. Boog Powell connected for a two-run blast in the fourth and Elrod Hendricks hit a bases-empty shot in the fifth inning to level the score at 3–3. The score remained the same through the top of the sixth. In the home half of the inning, Cincinnati appeared to have a rally started.

Ken Burkhart was behind the plate for Game One and had had few complaints going into the bottom of the sixth. With Reds at first and third with one out, Burkhart's serene day would quickly come to a turbulent climax. Ty Cline, a lefthanded hitter who had been acquired from Montreal earlier in the season, stepped into the batter's box. Palmer threw and Cline's swing hit the top of the ball, sending it almost straight down onto the plate. The ball bounced high into the air. "It was up fifteen or twenty feet," catcher Elrod Hendricks said after the game, "and I just prayed it would hurry down." Hendricks moved out of the catcher's box to play the ball, which was still high in the air near the third base line, about eight feet from home plate. Sensing that the ball might be foul, umpire Burkhart moved out beside Hendricks to make the call. Both Hendricks and Burkhart forgot about the Cincinnati runner on third base, Bernie Carbo, who was barrelling toward home plate with the potential go-ahead run.

Hendricks caught the ball in his catcher's mitt just inches fair. Burkhart signalled "fair ball" just as Hendricks transferred the ball to his throwing hand. Oblivious to Carbo, Hendricks was about to fire the ball to first base to retire Cline. Pitcher Jim Palmer, realizing that Carbo was nearing the plate, yelled at Hendricks, "Tag him! Tag him!" Hendricks, now aware of Carbo's intentions, whirled around to make the tag, only to come into contact with Burkhart, who had stayed put after his "fair" call. The force of Hendricks' turn knocked the umpire to the ground. Hendricks lunged over the fallen Burkhart and tagged Carbo with his empty mitt (the ball was still in his throwing hand) as Carbo attempted a hook slide around the two men. Burkhart, flattened by Hendricks, did not see any of what occurred. Nevertheless, while still on the turf, he signalled that Carbo was out.

Carbo, enraged at the idea that Burkhart had made a blind guess on the play, charged back up the line to confront the beleaguered umpire. By accident, Carbo stepped on home plate on his way to argue the decision. It was the only time during the sequence of events that the Cincinnati runner actually touched the plate; his slide around both Hendricks and Burkhart had caused him to miss the plate the first time. Cincinnati manager Sparky Anderson, amazed at what had just taken place, separated Carbo from the umpire. "I'd like to see the pictures of that one," Anderson informed Burkhart. "So would I," replied the umpire.

Although the television replays definitively showed that Burkhart was simply guessing to make his call, the umpire insisted he had seen enough of what had happened to make a judgment. "I looked over my shoulder and saw the catcher dive and tag him. It happened so fast I don't know how I saw it, but I did." Amazingly, Hendricks was also convinced he had legally tagged Carbo as he slid by. "When I caught the ball, the first thing I saw was the umpire. I ran into him and my momentum carried me over the top. That's when I tagged Carbo. If I had any doubts I would have tagged him again because he missed the plate." Burkhart stood by his "out" call and the bungled play came to an end. Cincinnati's apparent rally also ended when the next batter, pitcher Gary Nolan, lined out to Paul Blair in center field.

Baltimore, feeling lucky to have escaped the mess at home plate without being scored on, tallied a key run in the top of the seventh. Brooks Robinson's solo home run not only gave Baltimore a 4–3 lead but also persuaded Sparky Anderson to lift Nolan from the mound. Clay Carroll pitched the remainder of the game for Cincinnati and allowed no runs, but the Reds could not score, either. Game One went to Baltimore, 4–3, thanks in part to Burkhart's behind-the-back call in the bottom of the sixth.

When the game ended, the media circus, which always accompanies a World Series game, descended on the players for their views on the play. Many had not realized that Hendricks had tagged Carbo with an empty glove. Nor did many know that Carbo had missed home plate. The hottest property became a series of wire photos from the Associated Press which clearly showed the play in its entire absurdity: Carbo foolishly running, Hendricks forgetting about Carbo, Burkhart also dismissing Carbo from his mind, Hendricks knocking down Burkhart, the tag with the empty mitt, the slide which missed home, Burkhart's shaky "out" call, and the subsequent argument during which Carbo finally touched home by sheer accident. If it hadn't been a World Series game, one might have figured it to be a Little League contest, and a badly played one at that.

One might have also assumed that Sparky Anderson would be the angriest man in Ohio, but he wasn't. With a bit of convoluted logic, Anderson defended Burkhart's call in a UPI release:

> I don't want any umpire out there to be crucified when he's not wrong. Burkhart was not wrong. Sure, the way the play developed, my man was safe. But if Burkhart's not there, it's a routine play and Carbo's out by ten feet. He called him out because he knew he blocked off Hendricks. We got beat 4–3 and I'm not mad at anybody. If we got a few more runs, no one would even be talking about this play. These umpires are honest and sincere and they're trying to do a good job. I'm not going to jump on them.

The remaining games of the 1970 World Series are remembered largely for Brooks Robinson making one defensive gem after another at third base for the Orioles. Baltimore won Game Two 6–5 and Game Three by a 9–3 score. The Reds avoided a four-game sweep by rallying in Game Four for a 6–5 win. In their final chance to wrap up the Series at home, Baltimore did just that, cruising to a 9–3 victory in Game Five, even though Cincinnati had opened up a 3–0 lead in the top of the first inning. The Orioles had redeemed themselves after losing to the Mets in the 1969 World Series, Brooks Robinson was rightly named the series' Most Valuable Player, and Ken Burkhart went down in history for making one of baseball's most notoriously awful calls. The 1970 World Series was Burkhart's third and final appearance in the Fall Classic.

Chapter 18

The Designated-Hitter Rule: A Move to Offense, or an Offensive Move? (1973)

Baseball is a game between two teams of nine players each.
—*The Official Rules of Baseball*, Rule 1.01

Every season we are subtly reminded, in an indirect way, that baseball touches our emotions like no other sport. What other sport could possibly continue to generate arguments, both pro and con, regarding a rule change that occurred in 1973? That's the season in which the American League, in its wisdom(?), adopted the designated-hitter rule, a rule which has distinctly separated the two major leagues ever since and has, for better or worse, entirely changed the complexion of the sport.

Take a look at the dramatic rule changes the other three major professional sports have adopted. In the late 1970s, the National Football League, in order to generate more offense, instituted a "no-chucking rule" beyond a five-yard area from the line of scrimmage. The idea behind the move was to allow the fleet-footed wide receivers to move downfield without being hindered. The game opened up dramatically. Long touchdown catches became common. Many of today's star receivers probably could not have excelled under the old conditions, when receivers were liberally jostled. Yet how many times do you hear football fans discuss the merits of the no-chucking rule? Almost never.

The National Basketball Association adopted its three-point shot line in 1979. Few can doubt that this had a tremendous impact on strategy and style of play. Before 1979, a six-point lead in the NBA was large. To even the score, the trailing team would have to score three baskets without being scored upon themselves. Now, with the three-point shot, it requires only two unanswered baskets to tie the game. This was a wholesale change in a sport that had gone along for three decades with only a two-point field goal. But apart from the initial season, when the effects of the new rule were widely debated, the discussion has ceased.

In 1976 the National Hockey League liberalized their formerly restrictive two-line offside rule. Before that season, no two-line pass could be played by a teammate, regardless of where the receiver was when the puck crossed the line. The rule change allowed a player to accept a two-line pass if he was behind the second line when the puck crossed it. The result was astonishing. Free-skating offensive hockey prevailed and cautious positional play became instantly obsolete. Nevertheless, few hockey afficionados ever initiate arguments regarding how the style of the game has changed since 1976, and most younger fans have no idea how restrictive the offside rule once was.

Now contrast this to baseball fans' endless debate about the merits of the designated-hitter rule. The mere mention of it is often enough to make a purist's blood boil. It's also a surefire way to open up debate between those who favor the American League game and those who adhere to National League tradition. An observer just learning about baseball could be excused for thinking that the designated-hitter rule had been instituted this past winter rather than during the Nixon administration.

The idea of adding a designated hitter—a player who bats instead of the pitcher and assumes no defensive position—actually predates the American League's implementation by almost 50 years. In 1927, Judge Kenesaw Mountain Landis, baseball's first and most powerful commissioner, suggested the idea of a "designated pinch hitter" in order to stimulate offense in the game. Apparently the old judge was tired of seeing hapless pitchers flail pathetically at three pitches before sitting down. Some sympathized with the judge, but most owners and fans were used to the idea of nine men on offense and the same nine on defense. The idea died, for a while.

Then the 1960s rolled around, and for some reason that baseball historians are unable to pinpoint, the delicate balance between the pitcher and the batter began to shift noticeably in favor of the fellow standing on the mound. Pitchers suddenly became the focal point of the game. Dominant hurlers such as Drysdale, Koufax, and Gibson were embarrassing the offense. Shutouts became more and more frequent in the daily box scores. Pitchers were controlling the game at the expense of batters. The 1966 Los Angeles Dodgers won the National League pennant with a team batting average of .256. That average would have been the second worst in the NL in 1950. The 1966 World Series indicated how powerless the Dodgers were, despite the fact that they were solid pennant winners. In four games against the Baltimore Orioles, the Dodgers managed to score just two measly runs. In the next two years, things got progressively *worse* for batters.

The year 1968 stands as a monument to hitting futility. The American League batting champion was Carl Yastrzemski. He won the crown with an anemic .301 batting average. Even more surprising was the fact that Yastrzemski won the title by a comfortable margin, finishing 11 points ahead of Oakland's Danny Cater. Compare that to the 1940 AL batting statistics, a season when Detroit's Hank Greenberg batted .340 and finished *fifth*. Pitchers stifling opponents became utterly predictable. In the NL in 1968, both Bob Gibson and Don Drysdale recorded five shutouts *each* within the space of a calendar month. Surely change was needed, and change was made. The height of the mound was lowered and the size of the strike zone reduced, and the game began to readjust to a more equal battle between hitter and pitcher.

Even though batting averages began to return to a more respectable level, the fear that the pitchers might once again dominate began to frighten owners. The rash of 1–0 games, once considered exciting, drove away paying customers from the turnstiles. Attendance dropped during the 1960s, and many owners blamed this downslide on the lack of offense. The old idea suggested by Judge Landis was resurrected, at least by the American League, and the owners gave it their approval. Beginning in the 1973 season, the designated hitter would be part of American League baseball.

The reaction was immediate and far from unanimous. Those who treasure baseball as a reflection of American tradition were appalled. The very first rule in the book, Rule 1.01, stating that baseball is a nine-a-side affair, was being mocked. What was next? Designated runners for lumbering catchers? Designated fielders for defensive players with hands of iron? Altering the basic concept of each player taking his cuts at the plate and his turn in the field was pure sacrilege to many fans. Of course, those supporting the change were equally vociferous. The fans, they claimed, were fed up with the sight of pitchers striking out. Why, some pitchers could just as well be declared automatic outs and save everybody a lot of time. Take Hank Aguirre—please! He was a joke at the plate. In 1962 he had managed to stroke two hits in 75 at-bats for a miserable .027 average. If Aguirre's batting statistics for 1964 and 1965 were combined (nine hits in 123 at-bats), his average would be .073. Was this the kind of baseball the purists were trying to retain? The reformers were quick to point out that there were other Hank Aguirres who had no idea what to do in the batter's box. Sandy Koufax may have been a gleaming star on the mound, but he was a flickering lightbulb on offense. His best batting average for a single season came in 1965, when he hit .177. Seven times in his career he recorded averages below .100. The worst offender of all, advocates of the DH pointed out, was Bob Buhl, who in 1962 set an all-time record for ineptness by going hitless in 70 at-bats. This type of situation should be relegated to history, crowed those who applauded the American League's efforts to modernize the game.

It doesn't take a rocket scientist to realize that statistics indicate that pitchers have traditionally been awful hitters at the major-league level. But does that mean they should not have to take their turn at the plate like any other player? Those who support the DH rule are forced to admit that the elimination of the pitcher as a batter has also produced a serious side effect—the loss of strategic managing.

Let's examine a fictitious scenario. It's the bottom of the sixth inning. The game is tied at 1–1. Two are out and a runner is standing on second base. Next up is the pitcher (we'll call him Smith), who is having a tremendous game on the mound. He isn't tiring and is in full control of his stuff. There is a problem, though. Smith, like most pitchers, isn't much of an offensive threat. Perhaps it would be better to remove Smith in favor of a pinch hitter to try to score the runner from second base. What will the manager decide to do? The fans begin to debate the advantages of letting Smith bat for himself over replacing him with a pinch hitter. It makes for great discussion. The wrong decision by a manager makes for spirited second-guessing by fans. This is an enjoyable aspect of the game. Obviously, this can occur only in a league which requires the pitcher to bat. This interesting problem cannot occur with the designated-hitter rule in effect. The American League robs the fans of the chance to play armchair manager in this situation.

Where did the idea that pitchers can't hit come from? It is rather baffling. Go to any Little League park on a Saturday morning and watch the game. In a great many cases, the boy who is the starting pitcher for a team is also its best hitter. The same often holds true throughout the high-school level of baseball. Then, for some reason, at the collegiate level and in the low minor leagues, good-hitting pitchers become a rare commodity. However, those who think all major-league pitchers are offensive albatrosses are forgetting the 1988 World Series. In Game Two, Orel Hershiser of the Dodgers shut out the Oakland A's 6–0. Not only did the modest Hershiser pitch a brilliant game, he got three hits himself!

There are many examples of pitchers throughout the history of baseball who were more-than-capable batsmen. Does the name Ned Garver ring a bell? Probably not, unless you are a surviving member of the St. Louis Browns Fan Club. Garver, a member of the Browns from 1948 to 1952, was not only one of the team's best pitchers but a better-than-average hitter. On the days he pitched, he batted sixth in the Browns' lineup! In 1951 he hit .305 — not bad for a harmless pitcher. How about Walter Johnson? When he was not blowing fastballs by opposing batters, he could often be found batting them by opposing infielders. In 1925, when Johnson was nearly

38 years old, he notched 42 hits in 97 at-bats for a whopping .433 batting average. Let's not forget Red Ruffing, a key member of the New York Yankees' pitching staff during the 1930s. In his career, Ruffing won 273 games. Undoubtedly some of whose wins were generated by his own bat. Ruffing knocked in 273 runs in his career, and was often used as a pinch hitter on the days he didn't pitch. If pitchers aren't supposed to be able to hit, someone forgot to mention this to Ruffing, Johnson, and Garver.

Certainly the above-mentioned pitchers are the exception to the established norm. But history also records pitchers who on one day were the equal of any player with a bat in his hands. One example is Tony Cloninger. On July 3, 1966, while pitching for the Atlanta Braves, Cloninger became the only player in National League history to hit two grand slam home runs in one game. This was obviously a freak occurrence (Cloninger was a .192 career hitter), but nevertheless it is a remarkable story. How about Rick Wise? On June 23, 1971, Wise tossed a no-hitter for the Phillies in Cincinnati. Wise helped his cause somewhat by blasting two home runs. If the Phillies had been polled after the game, how many do you think would have supported the designated-hitter rule? "None" would probably be a safe answer. And finally, let us not forget the lesson taught to us by one George Herman Ruth. As a pitcher for the Boston Red Sox, Ruth connected for a total of nine home runs in 1915, 1916 and 1917. This was considered strange until someone (Boston manager Ed Barrow) thought that maybe the Babe could actually do more than pitch, and placed him in right field on the days he wasn't used on the mound. All Ruth managed to do was hit 714 career homers and revolutionize the sport. It is truly frightening to think that Ruth's batting talents may have gone undiscovered if the American League had used the designated-hitter rule in 1918.

The opponents of the designated-hitter rule continue to attack from all angles, and occasionally come up with a new one. Tony Kubek, during a pregame show on NBC's *Game of the Week* telecast, suggested that because they are not removed for pinch hitters like their National League counterparts, American League pitchers may be suffering from "DH burnout," which, according to Kubek's research, was shortening the career of the average AL hurler. Even

Reggie Jackson, a man who spent the latter years of his career as a DH, had reason to dislike the rule. "Normally," said Jackson, quoted in *Sports Illustrated*, "when a player hits a home run, he could look forward to running out to his position at the end of an inning to tip his cap to the crowd. What's a DH supposed to do? Tip his cap to the water cooler?"

Chapter 19

No Interference? The Armbrister-Fisk Collision (1975 World Series)

> It is interference by a batter or a runner when he fails to avoid a fielder who is attempting to field a batted ball. . . . When a catcher and batter-runner going to first base have contact when the catcher is fielding the ball, there is *generally* no violation and nothing should be called.
>
> —*The Official Rules of Baseball*, Rule 7.09 (1)

Among the most fondly remembered World Series ever played was the terrific seven-game thriller in the autumn of 1975, when the Cincinnati Reds and the Boston Red Sox tangled in a titanic contest that many observers credit with rekindling fan interest in baseball, which had been waning since the late 1950s. All the ingredients necessary for a high-class World Series were there: two well-known ball clubs with a surplus of big-name stars, franchises with colorful histories (both of which had gone abnormally long without a World Series winner), and close, nail-biting games with plenty of incidents to discuss if you happened to be part of the huge television audience that NBC was drawing to each of the seven games. One specific incident which was hotly debated at the time and still generates conflicting opinions today, even from the umpiring profession, was a call—or, more correctly, the lack of a call—by American League umpire Larry Barnett in the tenth inning of Game Three. Barnett's famous (or infamous, depending on your team allegiance) "no interference" call certainly played a major role in the Reds' victory that evening, and some say it may have deprived the Red Sox of their first World Series title since 1918.

The 1975 season had been a breakthrough year for both the Reds and the Red Sox, each in a slightly different way. Cincinnati had last won a World Series in 1940, and it took them another 21 seasons before they were National League champions again. The drought was broken in 1961, but the Reds fell in five games to the powerful New York Yankees in the World Series. Another nine years went by before the Reds made it to the big show again, where they were quickly dispatched by the Baltimore Orioles in five games in the World Series made famous by Brooks Robinson's dazzling defensive play at third base for Baltimore. Two years later, Cincinnati had another opportunity to clinch the elusive title as world champions, but lost in seven competitive games to Charlie Finley's mustachioed Oakland A's. The next year, 1973, ended bitterly for the Reds when they were the victims of an upset by the New York Mets in the National League Championship Series. In 1974, the Reds fell even further and failed to capture their division, finishing four games behind Walter Alston's Los Angeles Dodgers. In 1975, Cincinnati finally seemed ready to live up to their potential. The Reds cruised to the NL West crown by a whopping 20 games over Los Angeles, and brushed by Pittsburgh in three easy games in the NLCS to earn a spot in the World Series for the third time in six seasons.

The frustration of Boston Red Sox fans was already legendary by the mid–1970s. The Sox were baseball's most successful club from 1903 (when Boston won the first modern World Series) through the war-shortened 1918 campaign. In that period, the Red Sox won five World Series titles and six American League championships. Only the New York Giants' refusal to participate in the 1904 World Series (see chapter 2) prevented the Sox from winning the World Series each time they won the AL pennant. When Red Sox owner Harry Frazee sold Babe Ruth to the Yankees in 1920 to finance, of all things, a theatrical production, the proverbial "curse of the Bambino" was born. The Red Sox did not win another American League pennant until 1946; that October, Boston lost the World Series in seven heartbreaking games to the St. Louis Cardinals. A highly questionable pitching choice cost the Red Sox the 1948 AL flag, when they lost a one-game playoff to Cleveland after both clubs ended the regular season tied for first place (see chapter 11). In 1949, the Red Sox held a one-game lead over the Yankees with two games left to play in the season; New York won both contests and the Red Sox were left to spend the winter wondering what had gone wrong. Not much more was heard from the Bostons until 1967, when the Red Sox won the "impossible dream" pennant, so called because they had risen from ninth place to first in the space of one year. But even that momentum was not enough for the Red Sox to clear the final hurdle—they lost the World Series in seven games to Bob Gibson and the St. Louis Cardinals. The 1972 season saw the Red Sox begin to show the promise of things to come, and 1975 proved to be the year of fruition. The Sox won the AL East championship by four and a half games over Baltimore and surprised the three-time defending World Series champion Oakland Athletics in three straight games in the ALCS. Both Cincinnati and Boston were entering the Series on a roll, with high expectations to end significant World Series frustrations.

The 1975 World Series opened at Boston's historic Fenway Park on Saturday afternoon, October 11, before a capacity crowd. Cincinnati manager Sparky Anderson was trying to gain any possible edge before Game One even began. He knew Boston manager Darrell Johnson was planning to start Cuban-born Luis Tiant on the mound for the opener. Tiant was famous for his herky-jerky pitching delivery, which he altered very little even when runners were on base. Anderson was not totally convinced that Tiant's delivery was legal, and hoped to persuade the umpiring crew to call balks against him. When his club arrived in Boston, Anderson ran into the umpiring crew at Fenway Park and offered to show them videotapes of Tiant's alleged illegal deliveries. Anderson, in reality, had no such tapes, and would have been chagrined if the umpires had taken him up on the offer. However, he accomplished his mission when Tiant was called for a balk early in the game, when the Reds had a runner at first. Anderson could hardly contain his laughter, but in the end it was Tiant and Johnson who laughed the loudest, as the Red Sox won Game One 6–0.

In Game Two, Boston starter Bill "Spaceman" Lee set aside his sometimes bizarre behavior (he once lit a bonfire in the Red Sox bullpen to chase away some mosquitoes) and entered the ninth inning with a 2–1 lead. However, three Cincinnati hits (including doubles by Johnny Bench and Ken Griffey) turned the game around in the ninth inning. The Reds won 3–2 and evened the World Series at one game apiece. Both clubs were heading to Cincinnati's Riverfront Stadium with the Reds fully aware that they were extremely fortunate not to be down two games to none.

Both teams turned up the offense in Game Three on Tuesday evening, October 14, in the first night game of the Series. Boston catcher Carlton Fisk, who would play a key role in the controversial "no interference" call, hit the first home run of the 1975 World Series in the top of the second inning to give the Red Sox a 1–0 lead. But by the fifth inning, Cincinnati's Johnny Bench, Dave Concepcion, and Cesar Geronimo had all homered, to put the Reds in front by a 5–1 score. Boston scored one run in the sixth, and Bernie Carbo, a former member of the Reds, hit a solo homer in the seventh to narrow the score to 5–3. The score remained that way until Boston's young right fielder, Dwight Evans, hit a clutch two-run home run in the top of the ninth to tie the score at 5–5. Boston had rallied from a four-run deficit to get back into the game, and appeared to have momentum on their side. Cincinnati failed to score in the home half of the ninth, forcing the game into extra innings. Boston could not score in the top of the tenth. The stage was set for a play in which a little-known utility player and an even lesser-known AL umpire would, for all intents and purposes, decide Game Three of the 1975 World Series.

Leading off the bottom of the tenth for the Reds was Cesar Geronimo, who hit a soft single into center field off Red Sox pitcher Jim Willoughby, the fifth Boston hurler of the game. Due up next for the Reds was relief pitcher Rawly Eastwick, who posed no real offensive threat. To no one's surprise, Sparky Anderson opted to replace Eastwick with a pinch hitter. It would be unheralded Ed Armbrister, a right-handed hitter who had had 27 at-bats in similar situations during the regular season. Armbrister was not known as a power hitter, and every person in Riverfront Stadium expected him to try to move Geronimo to second base with a sacrifice bunt.

As expected, when Willoughby went into his windup, Armbrister squared around in the batter's box in position for a bunt. Armbrister made contact with the ball, but it was not a good bunt. The ball bounced straight in front of the plate and rebounded high off the hard dirt. Armbrister was slow getting out of the box, momentarily pausing to watch the ball. Boston catcher Carlton Fisk reacted more quickly and moved forward to field the ball, which was only a couple of feet in front of home plate. As Fisk was about to field the ball, Armbrister finally moved out of the batter's box toward first base. In doing so, he collided with Fisk, who was now slightly in front of him. The contact hindered Fisk momentarily, but the catcher still managed to grab the ball with his bare throwing hand. Armbrister was now in front of Fisk, who set himself to throw to shortstop Rick Burleson at second base in an attempt to force out Geronimo. Fisk's throw was well off the mark, and it sailed over Burleson's head into center field. Geronimo, who had slid going into second, regained his feet and safely advanced to third base. Armbrister rounded first and was standing on second base when the strange play finally ended.

In the visitors' dugout, Boston manager Darrell Johnson didn't even wait for the play to end before he started screaming at plate umpire Larry Barnett: "Interference, damn it!" He came onto the field to confront Barnett and ask him why he had failed to rule interference on Armbrister. (If Barnett had done so, Armbrister would have been declared out and Geronimo would have had to return to first base.) Barnett, who was probably the calmest man in the stadium, attempted to explain to Johnson that, although there was indeed a collision, the rules allow for minor contact between a batter and a catcher on bunt plays. Johnson, of course, was not buying it, and claimed that Armbrister's collision was severe enough to hamper Fisk's ability to make the play. "He [Armbrister] was all over the catcher!" Johnson shouted at Barnett, who stood fast with his original decision. Johnson then tried to persuade the other members of the umpiring crew to change the verdict. This, needless to say, was unsuccessful. Joe Morgan ended the game with a single to center field that scored Geronimo and gave the Reds a controversial 6–5 victory and a two-games-to-one lead in the Series. Undoubtedly, Armbrister's bunt was the key play of the game, and reporters eagerly asked members of both teams for their opinions. Darrell Johnson, feeling Barnett's inaction had cost his club a crucial game, was more than happy to oblige:

> We got a bad call. Armbrister clearly interfered with Fisk, which means he should have been automatically out. I got no satisfaction from the umpire, but replays will definitely show interference.

Barnett, describing the bunt to members of the media, remained placid and analytical:

> I ruled that it was simply a collision. It is interference only when the batter intentionally gets in the way of the fielder [on such a play]. I signalled that the ball was fair and in play. —Associated Press

Many Red Sox players were not convinced, and took their disagreement with Barnett to another level. Some suggested that major league baseball review its policy of awarding World Series umpiring assignments on a rotation basis and return to the days when merit was the sole factor in deciding which men would work the games. "If we're not going to have the best umpires," reasoned one player, "why should we have the best teams in the World Seires? Maybe the San Diego Padres and the Chicago White Sox should be playing here!"

The controversy was the talk of baseball fans across the continent, but thankfully the remainder of the Series contained enough thrills to divert most fans' attention from the tenth inning of Game Three. Luis Tiant pitched the Red Sox to a complete-game 5–4 victory in Game Four. Cincinnati won Game Five 6–2 and traveled to

Boston for Game Six, hoping to end the Series then. Boston would not cooperate, though, and won 7–6 in 12 innings on Carlton Fisk's famous home run, which he "convinced" to stay fair with some exaggerated body English. The Reds had led 6–3 going into the bottom of the eighth inning, but a three-run home run by Bernie Carbo had tied the score in the memorable contest. Some longtime baseball observers declared that Game Six of the 1975 World Series was the best game ever played, period.

Early in Game Seven, the Red Sox seemed to feed off the euphoria of Game Six's comeback and led 3–0 after five innings. Tony Perez, Cincinnati's dependable first baseman, hit a two-run homer in the top of the sixth to narrow Boston's lead to 3–2. A Cincinnati run in the seventh tied the score, and Joe Morgan's clutch RBI single in the ninth gave the Reds a 4–3 lead which they would not relinquish. Boston failed to score in the bottom of the ninth, giving Cincinnati its first World Series crown in 35 years. The curse of the Bambino was still haunting Fenway Park, the Red Sox, and their faithful followers.

Larry Barnett's call in Game Three, one based solely on judgment, certainly was responsible for the Reds winning that one game, but whether it had lingering effects on the whole Series is debatable. Barnett claimed it was "simply a collision" and so it stayed. Cincinnati, over a long season, had proven to be a great team, the best in baseball. A reporter asked flaky Boston pitcher Bill Lee if he agreed with that assessment. "No," deadpanned Lee. "The Taiwanese Little Leaguers have the best team."

Chapter 20

A Flip of the Hip: Did Reggie Jackson Commit Interference? (1978 World Series)

> It is interference by a batter or runner when any batter or runner who has just been put out hinders or impedes any following play being made on a runner. Such runner shall be declared out for the interference of his teammate.
> —*The Official Rules of Baseball*, Rule 7.09 (f)

When a baseball fan mentions the name of Reggie Jackson, throngs of images are likely to appear in one's mind. There was the titanic home run Reggie hit at Tiger Stadium in the 1971 All-Star Game, the ball majestically sailing over the upper deck in right field and deflecting off an electrical transformer. There was also the glorious October evening in 1977 when Reggie blasted three home runs in a World Series game, a feat previously accomplished only by Babe Ruth. Of course, there was the long-running feud with Yankees manager Billy Martin, highlighted by the televised shouting match between the two in the visitors' dugout at Fenway Park.

Fans of the Los Angeles Dodgers have another reason to remember Reggie Jackson. Already irked by Reggie's three homers against them in the 1977 Series, Dodgers fans were absolutely livid the following October when Jackson struck again, this time in a more subtle way. Those who bleed Dodger blue, from manager Tommy Lasorda down to playground urchins, strongly feel that a well-placed hip movement from Reggie Jackson played a strong role in the Yankees' victory over Los Angeles in the 1978 World Series.

Those who expected the 1978 World Series to be an ordinary affair had not been paying attention all season. The Series was simply a continuation of an improbable season in which the Yankees had been declared dead on more than one occasion yet managed to rise above the odds to squeak by the Boston Red Sox in dramatic fashion. Seemingly the team of destiny, the Yankees fed off their own momentum to gain victories in both the American League Championship Series and the World Series. It all looked so easy, but it was far from it. Common sense dictated that the Boston Red Sox were unbeatable in the summer of 1978. With a lineup that boasted the likes of Jim Rice, Carlton Fisk, Dwight Evans, and Fred Lynn, by the All-Star break the Bosox had rolled away from the rest of the pack in the AL East with an apparently insurmountable lead. The Yankees, despite being in third place with a 52–42 record, were in a state of turmoil. Omnipresent owner George Steinbrenner, unsatisfied with his club's performance, dumped manager Billy Martin, blaming Martin's confrontational personality for the Yankees' woes. After Dick Howser had acted as interim manager for one game, Steinbrenner gave the managerial reins to Bob Lemon, better known to an earlier generation of baseball fans as a star pitcher for the Cleveland Indians in the early 1950s.

For whatever reason—Martin's leaving or Lemon's coming or a combination of the two—the Yankees played winning, consistent baseball for the rest of the season. Boston, whose lead had been a comfortable 13½ games on July 21, stumbled through a losing streak, but managed to rebuild its lead to 8½ games on August 20. The Yankees kept right on winning, putting pressure on the frazzled Bosox. Boston went into another tailspin in the first half of September, losing 14 of 17 games. In that period, the Red Sox were routed by the Yankees in a series sweep at home, in what became known as the Boston Massacre. The worst fears of the Fenway faithful became reality. The Red Sox and the Yankees were locked in a virtual tie for the division title. This was not a positive omen for the good people of Boston. History had shown them, on several occasions, that a charging team in Yankee pinstripes often meant bad news for the Red Sox.

With the end of the schedule in sight, the Yankees pulled ahead of the Red Sox by three and a half games. Boston regrouped for one final effort. On the final day of the season, one game separated the front-running New Yorkers from the Red Sox. Boston knocked off the lowly Toronto Blue Jays and spent some anxious moments watching the Cleveland Indians, by no means a powerhouse, upend the Yankees. The 162-game schedule was over, and the Yankees and the Red Sox were tied for first place with 99–63 records. For the second time in American League history, a one-game playoff would be needed to settle a pennant race. The Red Sox won a coin toss and would host the memorable game, scheduled for the afternoon of Monday, October 2, 1978.

There was no point in trying to get any business done in the New England area that afternoon. Few people were at work, and many of those who did show up were clearly more interested in the portable radios and television sets they had brought along. High schools reported truancy rates so high that some wondered why the schools were open at all. It seemed that all of Massachusetts had shut down to watch the most important baseball game to be played at Fenway Park—depending on one's perspective—in three years, or in 11 years, or in its entire history. But there was not a sense of optimism in Boston—more of a sense of dread. Almost everyone had conceded the pennant to the Bosox in July. A win in the playoff game would only serve to solidify what should have been a foregone conclusion. A loss, or the mere thought of it, was utterly intolerable.

Boston got off to a 1–0 lead in the second inning, when Carl Yastrzemski hit a Ron Guidry fastball just inside the right-field foul pole. Surely, it was meant to be. The Red Sox very nearly blew the game wide open in the sixth, but were held to just one run. Lou Piniella, in right field for New York, snuffed out Boston's big inning with a desperate catch of a Fred Lynn line drive to keep the

Yankees in the game. Still, Boston held a 2–0 lead after six innings. Red Sox starter Mike Torrez, who suffered badly during the September losing streak, was pitching a fine game.

In the top of the seventh the Yankees got two runners aboard, but with two outs, harmless number-nine hitter Bucky Dent stepped in the batter's box. With the count at one ball, Dent fouled the next offering off his foot. He cracked his bat and on-deck hitter Mickey Rivers gave him a new one. On Torrez's next pitch, Dent swung and lifted a high arching shot toward the left-field wall. In Yankee Stadium or any other park, the ball would have been catchable. But this was Fenway Park, and the ball sailed above the 37- foot wall into the netting: a home run. The Yankees, despite being outplayed, led 3–2. Years later, Rivers revealed that he handed Dent a corked bat.

Before the top of the seventh ends, the Yankees upped their lead to 4–2. A Reggie Jackson home run in the eighth made it 5–2. The Red Sox refused to capitulate, however, and tallied two runs in the bottom of the eighth. The New York lead was now only 5–4. Boston tried to rally in the bottom of the ninth. With one man on and one out, Jerry Remy hit a line drive toward Piniella in right field. Piniella, obviously struggling with the sun, had trouble finding the ball, and it bounced in front of him. With a last-moment darting motion, Piniella grabbed the ball, which could have easily eluded him. A Jim Rice fly ball was responsible for the second out. With runners now at first and third, Yastrzemski faced vaunted Yankees reliever Goose Gossage. A high pop-up was the result, Graig Nettles making the catch in foul territory. New York won, 5–4. They had won 48 of 68 games under Bob Lemon. For the Red Sox and their devoted fans, it was another in a long string of disappointments and heartbreaks.

The win over Boston propelled the Yankees into the American League Championship Series for the third straight year. And for the third straight year, their opponents were the Kansas City Royals, who were proving to be the best of an inferior bunch in the AL West. In 1976 and 1977, the Yankees had struggled with the gritty crew from Missouri, each year needing their final turn at bat in the deciding fifth game to win the series. The 1978 ALCS proved to be a little bit more comfortable for New York. This time victory came three games to one and it earned them their third straight trip to the World Series. In 1976, Cincinnati had rolled over New York in four games. In 1977, New York had won its first World Series since 1962, beating the Dodgers in six games. With Los Angeles knocking off Philadelphia in the 1978 NLCS, the stage was set for another Dodgers-Yankees World Series.

The Dodgers and the Yankees were both well stocked with marquee players. New York had Reggie Jackson, Thurman Munson, Ron Guidry, Graig Nettles, and Goose Gossage. Los Angeles countered with Steve Garvey, Ron Cey, Davey Lopes, Tommy John, and Don Sutton. The first two games of the 1978 World Series were played at Dodger Stadium. The home team delighted their rabid fans by taking both of them, by scores of 11–5 and 4–3. The series shifted to New York, where the Yankees hoped the familiar confines of Yankee Stadium, plus the strong arm of Ron Guidry, could get them back in the running. Guidry did pitch a complete game in Game Three and the Yankees won 5–1, but the star of the night was Yankees third baseman Graig Nettles, who made four outstanding defensive plays which may have prevented seven Dodger runs from crossing the plate. Guidry, who had won 25 games during the season (including the playoff at Fenway Park), did not have his best stuff, but with Nettles at third base he didn't need it.

Game Four would prove to be the turning point in the Series. Ed Figueroa and Tommy John were pitching shutouts through the fourth inning. A three-run homer by the Dodgers' Reggie Smith in the top of the fifth gave Los Angeles a huge 3–0 lead, which they carried into the bottom of the sixth. With Roy White at second base and Thurman Munson at first, Reggie Jackson singled into right field, scoring White and advancing Munson to second. The score was now 3–1 and Lou Piniella was the batter. The Dodgers' lead now seemed approachable. The sellout crowd at Yankee Stadium grew louder as they sensed the drama unfolding. What they were about to see was one of the most controversial baserunning incidents in World Series history.

Piniella hit a sinking line drive toward Dodgers shortstop Bill Russell near second base. Russell appeared to have the ball momentarily in his glove, which was held ankle-high. The ball then squirted loose. Russell picked it up, stepped on second to force out Jackson, and then threw the ball toward first base for a double play. Jackson, already out, stood motionless between the throw and Dodgers first baseman Steve Garvey. With a slight, almost imperceptible movement of his hip, Jackson deflected the ball into right field. Garvey stopped for a moment to argue with first-base umpire Frank Pulli, and then chased the ball as Munson scored to make it 3–2. *New York Times* correspondent Joseph Durso described the incident this way:

> Piniella rammed a low line drive to shortstop with Thurman Munson on second base and Reggie Jackson on first. Bill Russell not only dropped the ball—which some people suspected was a shrewd bit of double-play strategy—but also fired it off Jackson's thigh while a critical run was crossing the plate.

Dodgers manager Tommy Lasorda sprinted from the dugout, shouting, "He's got to get out of the way!"—obviously referring to Jackson. Frank Pulli and second base umpire Joe Brinkman ruled that Jackson standing between Russell and Garvey did not constitute interference. This did not satisfy Lasorda, who maintained, "It had to be interference because Jackson's got to get out of the way." The umpires' interpretation of the rule was correct—interference occurs in this situation only when it is *intentional*—but what they had failed to notice was Jackson's subtle hip movement, which had redirected the ball into right field. Umpire Pulli later commented on Jackson's action in a *New York Times* article:

> From the angle I had at first base, I couldn't tell if Reggie went out of the line and so I called no interference. There was confusion on the play, so I looked at Joe Brinkman and he didn't give any sign.

A nation of baseball fans tuned into NBC's television coverage of Game Four were shown slow-motion replays. On the videotape, slowed down into fractions of seconds, there was little doubt that Jackson had deliberately interfered with Russell's throw.

The Dodgers escaped the sixth inning still clinging to a 3–2 lead. The Yankees eventually tied the score in the eighth and won it 4–3 in ten innings. Jackson's creative baserunning had switched the momentum of the whole Series. The Yankees walloped the Dodgers 12–2 in Game Five. If the Dodgers hoped the return trip to Los Angeles for Game Six would restore their good fortune, they were mistaken. New York rolled to a 7–2 win and took the 1978 World Series four games to two.

Dodgers fans, upset with their club's second consecutive loss to the Yankees in the World Series, were quick to point to the sixth inning of Game Four and Jackson's inconspicuous and uncalled interference as the torpedo which sunk the Dodgers' ship. Yankees fans were equally quick to retaliate, saying that Russell, on the same play, was himself guilty of breaching the rules by intentionally dropping Piniella's line drive and trying to turn it into a double-play grounder. Russell has escaped the controversy largely unscathed, but it was actually the Dodgers shortstop who created the controversy. Russell could easily have tagged Munson and stepped on second base for what would have been a much simpler double play. Instead, Russell opted to allow Munson to go to third, force out Jackson at second and throw to Garvey at first in an attempt to put out Piniella.

Nevertheless, Jackson had violated one of the game's baserunning rules. Since he had already been put out by Russell touching second base, his act of interference should have meant that Piniella was also out at first base, and Munson would have had to return to second. Unfortunately for the Dodgers, neither Frank Pulli nor Joe Brinkman saw Jackson's bit of chicanery. Only millions of television viewers did.

Chapter 21

A Half-Baked Idea Burns the Reds: Cincinnati and the 1981 Split Season

> Commissioner Bowie Kuhn cheated the players and fans out of a meaningful pennant race. He force-fed everyone a split season with an insane playoff system.
>
> —*The Baseball Hall of Shame* (Bruce Nash and Allan Zullo), summarizing Bowie Kuhn's short-sighted solution to the 1981 players' strike

The 1981 major league players' strike, which shut down America's national pastime for 59 days during the heart of the season, was the worst calamity to befall the sport since the Black Sox scandal made waves in 1920. In dealing with the game-fixers in 1919, major-league baseball appointed a commissioner, Kenesaw Mountain Landis, whose firm stance against corruption renewed public confidence in the sport. By comparison, when the 1981 players' strike threatened to ruin the credibility of an entire season, Commissioner Bowie Kuhn did what most believed to be impossible: he made a bad situation worse. Looking at the strike as a means of including an extra round of playoff games, Kuhn made a mockery of the traditional pennant races and ended up cheating a couple of teams out of their rightful divisional championships. The biggest victim of Kuhn's meddling ended up being the Cincinnati Reds. The Reds, who posted baseball's best overall record during the crazy 1981 season, were snubbed when it came to doling out the playoff invitations, a ridiculous situation which tainted the post-season.

Twice before 1981, major-league baseball fans had endured the predicament of their favorite players walking the picket line. In 1972, the first 13 days of the regular season had been canceled while the players and owners tried to hammer out their grievances. In 1980, eight days of the exhibition season were wiped out under similar circumstances. Besides being longer, the 1981 strike was infinitely worse, coming in the middle of a season which had been chock full of pleasant surprises. A rookie pitcher from Mexico, Fernando Valenzuela, had come out of nowhere to post one shutout victory after another for Los Angeles. Another rookie, Montreal outfielder Tim Raines, was stealing bases at an alarming rate. Not only was the rookie record for steals within Raines' grasp, Lou Brock's major-league mark of 118 for a season was as well. Milestones were also on the horizon for a veteran player or two. Pete Rose, now hustling in a Phillies uniform, was edging closer to the National League record for base hits, 3,630, established by Stan Musial. Steve Garvey had his sights set on Lou Gehrig's "iron man" record of 2,130 consecutive games played. If Garvey was to match the lofty standard set by Gehrig four decades earlier, he would have to appear in every game through the 1985 season, but as each game was entered into the scorebook, Gehrig's mark did not appear as out of reach as it had once looked.

The entire strike issue focused on the players' right to free agency, that is, their right to freely sign with another club as soon as their contracts with their present clubs expired. The possibility of free agency had been a reality for the players only since 1975, when the courts ruled that the traditional reserve clause in players' contracts (which bound players to their clubs in perpetuity) was invalid. Fearing that waves of players jumping from team to team at the end of each season would not be in the best interests of the sport, the players and owners had tentatively agreed to limit free agency. Teams who lost free agents were compensated with minor-league prospects from the teams who signed them. The players squawked that arrangements such as these infringed upon their capacity to negotiate salaries with other teams. They were right. The owners maintained that unchecked free agency would send salaries skyrocketing. They, too, were correct. With neither side ready or willing to compromise, June 12, 1981, loomed as a big date on the baseball calendar. That was the players' deadline. If a new arrangement regarding free agents was not on paper by June 12, the players had vowed to walk. Most fans were unwilling to believe such a scenario was possible.

June 12 did arrive, without any headway having been made between the owners and players. News broadcasters announced the sorry story to a disbelieving nation: the baseball season was on hold until the matter regarding free agency was settled. Few fans actually cared about the issues. They were just annoyed by what they perceived as a ridiculous situation. Major-league ballplayers on strike? What would be next, the football players from the NFL?

The strike generated several human-interest stories. First, Pete Rose had tied Stan Musial's NL hit record on the final day before the strike with a hit off Nolan Ryan. The public relations department of the Phillies had inflated 3,631 helium balloons, to be released as soon as Rose surpassed Stan the Man. With the strike in effect, the Phillies released them from an empty Veterans Stadium. Oakland's Mitchell Page became the happiest person in the history of baseball to be demoted to the minor leagues. Sent to Tacoma of the Pacific Coast League only days before the strike, Page was collecting his major-league salary. The reverse happened to pitcher Brad Havens, who had just been promoted from Orlando to the Minnesota Twins. Instead of getting a minor-league salary of $1,700 a month, Havens was now getting nothing. A number of stories centered on those who weren't players but still depended upon major league baseball for their livelihoods. John Henzl, the organist at Chicago's Wrigley Field, arrived at the park for the Cubs' June 13 game against the San Diego Padres. Nobody had bothered to notify Henzl of the strike, and the organist played for 30 minutes, oblivious of the empty stadium, before he was told to go home. Augie

Schmitt of the Houston Popcorn and Supply company was wondering what on earth he was supposed to do with the 100,000 pounds of peanuts he had in cold storage. "Suppose the Astros don't play the rest of the year?" he wondered. "What am I going to do—eat them myself?" Despite these hardships, the strike churned on through the month of July. Fans were fondly looking back at the standings of June 12, the last time teams in major-league uniforms had taken the field. The way the clubs stood on June 12, although nobody realized it at the time, would have a major bearing on the rest of the season.

MAJOR LEAGUE STANDINGS, JUNE 12, 1981

American League East

Team	W	L	GBL
New York	34	22	-
Baltimore	31	23	2
Milwaukee	31	25	3
Detroit	31	26	3½
Boston	30	26	4
Cleveland	26	24	5
Toronto	16	42	19

American League West

Team	W	L	GBL
Oakland	37	23	-
Texas	33	22	1½
Chicago	31	22	2½
California	31	29	6
Kansas City	20	30	12
Seattle	21	36	14½
Minnesota	17	39	18

National League East

Team	W	L	GBL
Philadelphia	34	21	-
St. Louis	30	20	1½
Montreal	30	25	4
Pittsburgh	25	23	5½
New York	17	34	15
Chicago	15	37	17½

National League West

Team	W	L	GBL
Los Angeles	36	21	-
Cincinnati	35	21	½
Houston	28	29	8
Atlanta	25	29	9½
San Francisco	27	32	10
San Diego	23	33	12½

On August 1, fans who had grown accustomed to the dismal reports of the player-owner negotiations were stunned to learn that a settlement had been reached. In a compromise, the players were granted a slightly better deal regarding free agency, while the owners would not be totally uncompensated for the loss of key players.

With the season ready to resume after the All-Star Game (which was hastily rescheduled, in Cleveland), the burning question was how the rest of the season would be handled. Many expected the schedule to be resumed and the lost games ignored. That was the sensible way of doing things, according to most observers. However, Commissioner Bowie Kuhn had other plans.

Kuhn deemed that the strike had created two seasons. The first season had ended on June 12, and the four clubs atop their division on that date were declared partial pennant winners. This came as quite a surprise to the Dodgers, Phillies, Athletics and Yankees, all of whom suddenly qualified for postseason play. Kuhn also announced that the remaining games on the schedule would constitute the second season, with the division winners in the first half playing those of the second half in four three-out-of-five series to determine which clubs would advance to the annual league championship series.

In theory, Kuhn's plan sounded good, but it did not take long for a few flaws to surface. The most irritating development arose when Kuhn announced that if a first-half winner also finished on top of its division in the second half, it would *not* receive a bye to the LCS. Instead, that team would be forced to endure a best-of-five series against the club in its division with the next-best cumulative record in both halves of the schedule. Immediately, warning alarms went off in the minds of those who enjoy dabbling with figures. Why, they asked, would a team such as the Yankees even try in the second half, when they already had a playoff spot guaranteed and could not improve their situation by trying for a first-round bye? Worse yet, some imaginative writers figured out ways in which a team could lose a late-season game and benefit by it. One of these loser-wins scenarios featured the Baltimore Orioles. Somebody ran the numbers and found out that if New York trailed Boston by half a game on the last day of the season, and the Orioles were solidly in third place, the Orioles would be wise to deliberately lose to New York. Why? If Boston were to win the second half, the Red Sox would play the Yankees in the intra-divisional playoff series. But if New York were to repeat as winners in the second half, they would play the AL East team with the next-best cumulative record: the

Baltimore Orioles! Managers Tony LaRussa and Whitey Herzog said they would either forfeit or deliberately dump a game in similar circumstances to gain a postseason berth. When statements such as those became public, Kuhn retreated and declared that if a club managed to win both halves of the pennant, it would indeed earn a bye to the LCS.

With the chance of strategic game-dumping eliminated, the second half of the season began. Among the happiest clubs was the Kansas City Royals. The Royals had won the American League pennant in 1980 and were favored to repeat in 1981. However, Kansas City got off to a dismal start and had won just 20 of 50 games before the strike. Mired in fifth place, 12 full games behind division-leading Oakland, the Royals would have needed a miracle to repeat as AL West champions in a normal season. However, 1981 was turning into a very abnormal campaign. The fresh start each team got beginning in August was the tonic that Kansas City needed. Other clubs were just as happy. Toronto, Minnesota, and the Chicago Cubs were on their way to establishing team loss records when the strike granted them a reprieve. When the second half of the split season began, all 26 major league clubs were at square one again. With about 50 games remaining on each team's schedule, anything was possible, including an injustice which would victimize the Cincinnati Reds.

Early in October the season ended. The second-half standings based solely on the season's final two months, read this way:

FINAL STANDINGS, 1981 SECOND HALF

American League East				American League West			
Team	W	L	GBL	Team	W	L	GBL
Milwaukee	31	22	-	Kansas City	30	23	-
Boston	29	23	1½	Oakland	27	22	1
Detroit	29	23	1½	Texas	24	26	4½
Baltimore	28	23	2	Minnesota	24	29	6
Cleveland	26	27	5	Seattle	23	29	6½
New York	25	26	5	Chicago	23	30	7
Toronto	21	27	7½	California	20	30	8½

National League East

Team	W	L	GBL
Montreal	30	23	-
St. Louis	29	23	½
Philadelphia	25	27	4½
New York	24	28	5½
Chicago	23	28	6
Pittsburgh	21	33	9½

National League West

Team	W	L	GBL
Houston	33	20	-
Cincinnati	31	21	1½
San Francisco	29	23	3½
Los Angeles	27	26	6
Atlanta	25	27	7½
San Diego	18	36	15½

As it turned out, no first-half winner repeated as second-half champion, so no byes were awarded. But not everyone was thrilled with the way things had worked out. The angriest cries came from Cincinnati. The Reds had not won either half, but they had still managed to put together a combined record of 66–42, the best cumulative record in all the majors. What was Cincinnati's reward? Nothing! Competing in the NL West playoffs would be Los Angeles and Houston, the clubs which had won the two halves. This was outrageous to Reds fans, who claimed that Houston's mediocre first half and the Dodgers' so-so second half did not measure up to Cincinnati's quality play throughout both halves of the schedule.

Many similar complaints were echoing from St. Louis. Like the Reds, the Cardinals did not finish first in either half of the NL East standings but had put together a solid combined season, better than either Montreal or Philadelphia, the two clubs who would be squaring off in the NL East playoff. The season was a cruel joke to both the Reds and Cardinals. The NL's two best clubs would miss postseason play because of an ill-conceived format foisted upon major-league baseball by Commissioner Bowie Kuhn.

When the eight-team post-season got rolling, Montreal beat Philadelphia, Los Angeles ousted Houston, the Yankees defeated Milwaukee, and Oakland swept Kansas City. In the League Championship Series, which normally would have opened postseason play, the New York Yankees had little trouble dispatching Oakland in three straight games. Los Angeles was forced to rally to eke out a three-games-to-two series victory over a pesky Montreal club. With momentum seemingly on their side, the Dodgers won their first World Series since 1965, knocking off the Yankees in six games.

Cincinnati fans, despondent over the cruel fate their team had suffered, maintained the Dodgers were tainted champions. Heck, L.A. wasn't even the best club in the NL West, they noted. How would the Reds have done against the Yankees? We'll never know, thanks to Bowie Kuhn and his silly split season.

Chapter 22

The Game That Refused to Die: The Great Pine-Tar Debate (1983)

> A batter is out for illegal action when he uses or attempts to use a bat that, in the umpire's judgment, has been altered or tampered with in such a way as to improve the distance factor or cause an unusual reaction on the baseball. This includes bats . . . covered with a substance such as paraffin, wax, etc.
>
> —*The Official Rules of Baseball*, Rule 6.06 (d)

> The bat handle, for not more than 18 inches from its end, may be covered or treated with any material or substance to improve the grip. Any such material or substance, which extends past the 18-inch limitation, shall cause the bat to be removed from the game.
>
> —*The Official Rules of Baseball*, Rule 1.10 (c)

On July 24, 1983, the Kansas City Royals were in Yankee Stadium to play the final game of a weekend series against the New York Yankees, a team battling with the Baltimore Orioles for the lead in the American League East. For eight innings, the Sunday afternoon crowd watched a highly competitive contest in which both teams held the lead at different stages. Each club scored a run in the second inning. The Royals got one more in the fourth and another in the sixth to open up a 3–1 advantage. However, three runs in the home half of the sixth turned the tables and the Yankees grabbed a 4–3 lead, a lead they clung to through the eighth inning. When the Royals came to bat in the ninth, they faced the formidable task of trying to scratch a run off Richard "Goose" Gossage, the Yankees' smoke-throwing closer, who had notched 101 saves from 1979 to 1982 and had earned the reputation of being baseball's premier relief pitcher. This alone was a daunting prospect, but the visiting Royals had no idea that their next half inning would stretch over a period of 25 days, involve two protests, two umpiring crews, litigation from disgruntled spectators, and result in a controversial ruling by the American League president, who declared that the letter of the law doesn't always apply.

The top of the ninth inning proceeded in a manner which all true fans of close ballgames enjoy. The Royals were mounting a serious threat to the tenuous 4–3 New York lead. Gossage was competent on the mound, but not his usual overpowering self. Still, he was doing his job—holding onto the slim one-run lead and recording outs. When George Brett, the Royals' star third baseman, stepped into the batter's box, the situation was this: two outs with a runner (U. L. Washington) on first base. Gossage's first pitch to Brett was a ball. Gossage checked the runner briefly, fired his trademark fastball toward the plate . . . and then the fun began!

Brett was anticipating Gossage's fastball. The pitch was high, but Brett's powerful swing met the ball solidly. From the moment contact was made, there was absolutely no doubt that the ball would clear the right field wall. It did, with plenty of room to spare, finally landing well back in Yankee Stadium's bleacher seats. Brett and Washington began to circle the bases to give the Royals an apparent 5–4 lead. However, Yankees manager Billy Martin wasn't ready to concede the home run just yet. He proceeded to act upon a plan that he had discussed with his coaches and catcher Rick Cerone a couple of weeks earlier. It had to do with what Martin perceived as an illegality with Brett's bat—the bat he had just used to swat the home run to give Kansas City the lead.

During an earlier road trip the Yankees had made to Kansas City, Martin began to get curious about the quantity of pine tar—the sticky natural substance which many hitters apply to their bats to improve the grip—that Brett was liberally smearing on the handles of his bats. Martin leafed through the rule book and discovered the two passages—Rules 6.06 (d) and 1.10 (c)—which outlined the penalties for the misuse of substances such as pine tar. Sensing an opportunity to use the rules to his advantage, Martin had secretly measured the amount of pine tar on each one of Brett's personal bats, and confirmed his suspicions that the applications of pine tar exceeded the maximum allowable length of 18 inches. Like a good gambler, Martin was prepared to wait until the best possible opportunity arose to divulge his knowledge. July 24, 1983, proved to be that opportunity.

So while the dejected Yankee Stadium crowd was moaning over the 5–4 lead the Royals were about to take, Martin was busily signalling to his catcher, Cerone, to seize Brett's bat, which was still lying in the batter's box. Recalled Cerone, "I originally began looking for cork. I tossed the bat down, then I remembered what I was supposed to be checking for." Kansas City's batboy tried to take the bat to the visitors' dugout, but Cerone grabbed it and then suggested to home plate umpire Tim McClelland that the bat was in violation of the rules and Brett should be declared out. Brett crossed home plate behind Washington, glanced back at the conversation Cerone and McClelland were having, and trotted toward his dugout. The high-fives and handshakes among the Royals stopped abruptly when they noticed that the umpiring crew had gone into a huddle with Brett's bat. After some discussion, the bat was placed lengthwise across the front of home plate. Knowing that the width of home plate is 17 inches, and seeing that the pine-tarred portion of Brett's bat was considerably longer, McClelland turned to the Royals' dugout and signalled that Brett was out and the game was over. New York had won by a score of 4–3.

In the annals of major league baseball there has probably never been an angrier player than George Brett was at that very moment. He charged wildly out of the dugout in an attempt to get at McClelland. Brett was intercepted by crew chief Joe Brinkman, who tried in vain to explain to Brett why his game-winning homer had been declared a game-losing out. The Royals weren't buying any of it and continued to verbally accost the four umpires while Yankees manager Billy Martin was grinning uncontrollably. When all the shouting had concluded, four members of the Royals (Brett, manager Dick Howser, coach Rocky Colavito, and pitcher Gaylord Perry) had been thumbed out of the game. The large crowd, not knowing precisely what had happened, cheered wildly and left the stadium under the impression that the home team had just won the game, although few could explain why.

The controversial bat was taken by the umpires into their dressing room for safekeeping. Brinkman had a hunch that the controversy was far from over. Meanwhile, in the Royals' locker room, the players and coaching staff continued to fume. "Broadway wouldn't buy this script," declared ejected manager Howser. "It wouldn't last past opening night, it's so unbelievable!" Howser, with the complete support of the Royals' ownership, filed a formal protest to the office of American League president Lee MacPhail.

Four long days passed before MacPhail handed down his decision. He knew that the umpires, according to the rules of the game, were absolutely correct in nullifying Brett's home run. But he also realized that by upholding the umpires' decision, he could be opening a floodgate of numerous other technicalities which would destroy the nature of the sport. It was an unenviable situation for MacPhail, considering his current home address was an apartment in New York City. In the interim, sportswriters and historians were researching the history of the rule, and concluded that the "pine tar rules" had been adopted during the mid–1950s more to prevent the balls from becoming sticky rather than to deprive batters of hits. On July 28, MacPhail announced his verdict. He declared that although Brett's bat was technically illegal, it did not violate "the spirit of the rules" and was therefore legal. The home run counted. Kansas City had taken a legitimate 5–4 lead, and the remainder of the game would be played on August 18, the next available open date for both teams.

Now it was the Yankees' turn to be outraged. Martin, who believed he had scored a major victory for rule-book readers, was livid.

First he mocked MacPhail's decision. "I didn't know the rules were spiritual," he stated. Martin then suggested the rule book is only good "when you go deer hunting and you run out of toilet paper." Omnipresent Yankees owner George Steinbrenner was even more menacing. He suggested that it wouldn't be wise for MacPhail to live in New York City if the Yankees happened to lose the American League East title by a one-game margin. "It [MacPhail's decision] sure tests our faith in our leadership," growled Steinbrenner. Predictably, the Royals applauded MacPhail and his use of common sense. Most experts agreed that Brett's hit had not been aided by the additional pine tar and certainly deserved to stand as a home run. The American League office hoped to put the entire episode to rest with the conclusion of the game on August 18, but "the game that refused to die," as it was now being called, had a few more twists and turns in it.

First, the August 18 resumption date created a problem. Playing on that date would make both teams violate the principle of playing no more than 18 consecutive dates without a day off. Since this was the only available date to conclude the July 24 game, the "day off" policy was ignored. Next, the Yankees decided that anyone who wanted to see the resumption of the game would have to pay $1 to sit in the bleachers or $2.50 for a grandstand seat. Season ticket holders would be exempt from this charge, but ticket stubs from July 24 would *not* be honored. Two angry ticketholders took umbrage at this pronouncement and went to court to prevent the game from being continued until the Yankees relented and allowed ticketholders from July 24 to be admitted to the August 18 continuation free of charge. A temporary injunction was granted. Eventually, the litigation reached all the way to the Appellate Division of the New York Supreme Court, where Justice Joseph P. Sullivan ordered the game continued with the declaration, "Play ball!"

Lee MacPhail tried to restore goodwill with the Yankee hierarchy with a luncheon shortly before the August 18 resumption date. He jovially suggested that the Yankees should have fun with the fans on August 18 and hinted that anyone who attends should be given a miniature of Brett's bat—coated with pine tar, of course. MacPhail observed that the Yankees were not in a laughing mood and might have a few tricks left up their sleeves. MacPhail left the lunch wondering what tactics the Yankees might try to discredit his decision—and took some extraordinary precautions.

When August 18 arrived, 1,245 spectators were present at the stadium for the game's conclusion. Most had willingly paid the small admission price even though the Yankees had relented and declared that anyone with a July 24 ticket stub would be admitted free. (This decision by New York management came very late, and few fans took advantage of the offer.)

The Yankees took their place on the field to conclude the top of the ninth. As a form of protest, Billy Martin had made two outrageous lineup changes. Pitcher Ron Guidry was stationed in center field. Don Mattingly, normally an outfielder or first baseman, was shifted to second base. Martin was letting everyone know that he considered MacPhail's decision to be a farce. Martin was now ready to play his trump card. Before pitcher George Frazier threw his first pitch to Hal McRae (who had been on deck for 25 days), he appealed to first base umpire Tim Welke that Brett had not touched first base on his home-run trot three and a half weeks earlier! "Safe!" said Welke. Undaunted, Frazier appealed that Brett had missed second base. "Safe!" said Dave Phillips.

Out of the dugout came Martin with his rehearsed argument. He seemed to have a valid complaint. How could this umpiring crew know if Brett had legally touched the bases? After all, they were in Seattle when Brett hit the ball! Much to Martin's amazement, Phillips produced a notarized letter, signed by the original umpiring crew, stating that both U. L. Washington and George Brett had indeed run the bases properly on July 24. In the Royals' bullpen, relief pitcher Dan Quisenberry was thoroughly impressed. "Whoever thought of that [letter] should be the next commissioner," said Quisenberry. (It was the brainchild of Lee MacPhail.) Martin was less than impressed, though, and protested this decision by proxy. Drew Coble, the July 24 first base umpire, theorized Martin, was watching Brett's hit fly over the fence, and had no business signing the letter. Martin said he was playing the game under protest. The twelve hundred fans cheered.

Hal McRae struck out to end the top of the ninth. The Yankees went down one-two-three in the bottom of the ninth. It had taken all of 12 minutes to complete the game.

Still Martin and the Yankees persisted. A formal protest was lodged with the American League office. Thankfully, it was rejected. The game was over. Final score: Kansas City 5, New York 4. The entire mess was best summed up by New York's Don Baylor, and quoted in *The Baseball Hall of Shame*, "If I had wanted to watch a soap opera, I'd have stayed at home."

Chapter 23

Bad Time for a Bad Call: Don Denkinger's Infamous Safe-at-First Call (1985 World Series)

> Any umpire's decision which involves judgment, such as . . . whether a runner is safe or out, is final. No player, manager, coach, or substitute shall object to any such judgment decisions.
>
> —*The Official Rules of Baseball*, Rule 9.02 (a)

When one totals up balls and strikes, safes and outs, fair balls and foul balls, it is not uncommon for an umpiring crew to have to make approximately 300 calls in each game. In 1985 there were 2,101 regular season games played in the major leagues (1,131 in the American League and 970 in the National League). Twenty more games were played in the post-season for a grand total of 2,121 major league games. Multiply that figure by 300. The total of 636,300 will give you some indication of how many judgment calls were made by major league umpires in 1985. Unfortunately for veteran American League umpire Don Denkinger, one of those calls was clearly incorrect. There are those who believe that lone call cost the St. Louis Cardinals the 1985 World Series.

By the time that Series ended, Denkinger's name had become widely known to baseball fans—particularly those who rooted for the Cardinals—in terms that were less than flattering. It was not fair to Denkinger, an American League crew chief, but such is the nature of the game: all the calls that are clearly correct generate no response from players or fans; it's the one that is flagrantly incorrect that places the umpire in hot water. Such was the situation Don Denkinger found himself in on October 26, 1985, and is still reminded of by fans who recall Game Six of the 1985 World Series as if it were yesterday.

There was no way, back in 1960, that Denkinger would have figured that one day he would be the most controversial man in America. Drafted into the army in 1957, he had just about finished his stint in the service when an army buddy, Bob Henrion, persuaded Denkinger to accompany him to Al Sommers' School for Umpires in Daytona Beach. As Denkinger later recalled, "I couldn't even fathom what it was an umpire was supposed to do." But, as a lark, he traveled to Florida with Henrion and immediately became fascinated with the idea of becoming a professional baseball umpire. To the shock of Henrion (and himself), Denkinger graduated at the top of his class and was voted most likely to succeed in the professional umpiring ranks. After the rigors of calling balls and strikes for eight years in the minor leagues, Denkinger was promoted to the American League in 1969, at the relatively young age of 32.

Denkinger loved his job. "I'm in a unique profession," he told *Sports Illustrated* in 1986, "one that people don't know a lot about. I know we have this hateful image, but it's totally untrue that we lead a miserable, lonely life. Why, I've got friends in every city we go to."

Like most successful umpires, Denkinger remained largely anonymous, but was being assigned to ever more prestigious games. He worked the 1971 All-Star Game at Tiger Stadium, the American League Championship Series in 1972, the World Series in 1974 and 1980. Denkinger became a well-respected community leader in his home town of Waterloo, Iowa, where he could always be counted on to assist in civic projects and charity work. In 1977 he was elevated to the position of crew chief, a sign that the American League was pleased with the job he was doing. He was on top of the world. The 1985 World Series would be another accomplishment to add to his résumé, he thought.

The 1985 baseball season could have done without a controversial finish; the season had already been strange enough. First, in a repeat of 1981, the players staged a mid-season strike, much to the horror of fans who four years earlier had suffered through a baseball-less July for the first time in 106 years. Thankfully, both players and management came to their senses after one day, and the schedule was resumed. The American League Championship Series pitted the Toronto Blue Jays, in their first-ever postseason appearance, against the Kansas City Royals. In seven games of miraculous comebacks and questionable calls, the Royals rallied from a 3–1 deficit in games to take the series and earn a place in their first World Series since 1980. In the National League, St. Louis pulled off a mild upset by knocking off Tommy Lasorda's Dodgers in six games, in a series which featured improbable home runs from the Cardinals' Ozzie Smith and Tommy Herr. This set the stage for a St. Louis–Kansas City World Series, the first time the World Series had featured two Missouri-based clubs since the Browns and Cardinals played in the all–St. Louis Series in 1944.

To those followers of the sport who believe that momentum is as critical to success as solid pitching, it would have appeared by the end of Game Two that St. Louis had a lock on the World Series. John Tudor got credit for the Cardinals' 3–1 road victory in Game One. The next night the Cards managed just two hits in eight innings off Kansas City's Charlie Leibrandt, but exploded for four hits in the ninth (including a bases-loaded double by Terry Pendleton) to score four runs. The final score was 4–2 for St. Louis, in a game the Cards clearly deserved to lose. St. Louis had taken the first two games at Kansas City. It was a positive omen. No team had ever lost the World Series after winning the first two games in the opponents' ballpark.

The Series shifted to St. Louis on October 22 for Game Three. Those expecting the Cardinals to continue their roll to the world championship were disappointed, as the Royals' young starter Brett

Saberhagen went the distance in a 6–1 Kansas City win. The Cards were back in control in Game Four, when John Tudor was even better than he had been in the series opener, pitching a complete-game 3–0 shutout. St. Louis now held a commanding lead of three games to one, with Game Five set for Busch Stadium. Kansas City was not ready to die, though, as they responded with a convincing 6–1 victory in Game Five. This time Danny Jackson was the mound hero for the Royals, allowing just five hits. The stage was set for Game Six, a nail-biting pitchers' duel that featured the routine ground ball which has come to haunt Don Denkinger.

Game Six was played on October 26 before a full house at Royals Stadium and a Saturday evening national television audience courtesy of ABC. For seven innings, St. Louis' Danny Cox and Kansas City's Charlie Leibrandt engaged in a classic battle. The score stood at 0–0 in the top of the eighth inning when the Cardinals began to put together the pieces of a rally. With two outs and St. Louis runners occupying second and first, Cardinals manager Whitey Herzog decided to gamble. Danny Cox was the next scheduled hitter, but Herzog opted to lift his starter in favor of a pinch hitter, little-used utility man Brian Harper. The move paid dividends for Herzog when Harper blooped a single into center field to put St. Louis ahead 1–0. Kansas City was shut out in the home half of the eighth. The Cardinals failed to add to their lead in the top of the ninth. Kansas City was down to their final three outs to try to even the score. As expected, Herzog summoned his closer, big Todd Worrell, from the bullpen to wrap up the game and the World Series. All through the 1985 season, the Cardinals had never lost a game in which they were leading after eight innings. Tonight would be different.

Leading off the bottom of the ninth for the Royals was left-handed pinch hitter Jorge Orta. Orta quickly fell behind oh-and-two. On the next pitch, Orta hit a slow roller off the end of his bat between Worrell and first baseman Jack Clark. Clark fielded the ball cleanly and flipped it to Worrell, who had moved over to cover first base. Orta looked like the first out, but Don Denkinger, the first base umpire, stationed eight feet from the bag in foul territory, called Orta safe.

Nobody on the St. Louis bench could believe it. Herzog rushed from the dugout to challenge the call. Worrell joined the discussion from the mound. There was no way Orta could not have gotten to the bag first, he insisted, because Orta stepped on the back of his foot after he, Worrell, had touched the bag. (Television replays confirmed Worrell's claim.) Denkinger, following standard practice for all judgment calls, stood by his original decision. Orta was safe at first base with none out.

The controversy left the Cardinals rattled. The next batter, Steve Balboni, lofted a high pop-up near the Royals' dugout. Clark moved over to make a routine catch. Amazingly, Clark lost sight of the ball, and it fell untouched to the turf. Balboni, given a second life, hit a single. Now there were Royals at first and second with none out. Jim Sundberg attempted to lay down a sacrifice bunt, but Worrell fielded the ball and threw to third base in time to force out Orta. Pinch hitter Hal McRae was the next batter. Worrell fired a slider that eluded Cardinals catcher Darrell Porter. The passed ball moved the runners to second and third. Herzog, managing by the book, ordered McRae intentionally walked to set up a force play. Dane Iorg, the last left-handed hitter on the Kansas City bench, entered the batter's box. After taking the first pitch inside for a ball, Iorg hit a broken-bat blooper into right field. Balboni scored easily from third, followed by Sundberg, who slid into home, safe. The Royals won, 2–1, tying the World Series at three games apiece.

In marked contrast to the celebrating Kansas City Royals was an angry group of Cardinals in the visitors' clubhouse. Herzog is quoted in *The Baseball Hall of Shame*: "It's bleeping unbelievable." "We're going to win the bleeping World Series and he boots that play." There was no mistaking which "he" Herzog was referring to: first-base umpire Don Denkinger. According to the standard umpires' rotation, Denkinger would work the plate for Game Seven. Herzog was well aware of this. "Now we've got the bleeper behind the plate tomorrow. We've got about as much chance as the man in the moon."

While the Royals were happy with their reprieve, the Cardinals, following Herzog's cue, were more in the mood for sulking than preparing for Game Seven. It clearly showed. After three innings,

Kansas City had built a comfortable 5–0 lead off St. Louis starter John Tudor. When Tudor was yanked in favor of a reliever he was so upset he punched an electric fan in the clubhouse, causing a nasty gouge on his hand. With the score 9–0 in the bottom of the fifth inning, Herzog lit the fuse for an ugly scene by bringing in hot-tempered Joaquin Andujar to pitch. Andujar immediately raged at Denkinger, after an obviously wide pitch was called a ball. Herzog charged out on the field, presumably to restrain his angry pitcher, but he also took the opportunity to verbally blast Denkinger. "We shouldn't even be out here tonight!" Herzog ranted. "You know you blew that call!" Denkinger had heard enough and ejected the St. Louis manager.

If Denkinger hoped to settle the volatile situation by disposing of Herzog, he was mistaken. Andujar's next pitch was clearly another ball, but Andujar was determined to pick a fight. He, too, was ejected. It was the first time a player and his manager had been tossed out of a World Series game in 50 years. Kansas City scored two more runs and won the game 11–0 and the Series four games to three. However, things were far from over for the Denkinger household.

Back in Waterloo, Iowa, Denkinger's wife and three teenage daughters were watching Game Seven on television. The girls became emotionally upset at seeing their father attacked by Herzog and Andujar. That was just the beginning. Angry and obscene telephone calls began pouring into the home. It seems that a disgruntled St. Louis radio personality had given Denkinger's home number over the air and encouraged his listeners to harass his family. A writer from the St. Louis *Post-Dispatch* took to referring to the beleaguered umpire as "Jesse James." Hate mail began to arrive at Denkinger's address, at first a small trickle, then bagfuls. Eventually, Denkinger asked the Waterloo post office to stop mail delivery altogether. Local police protected the Denkinger home for a while. It was not a pleasant situation.

Sports Illustrated, in its report on the World Series, tried to deflect criticism from Denkinger and place it on the shoulders of the Cardinals. The magazine pointed out that Balboni's dropped pop-up and Porter's passed ball were at least as much to blame for the Cards' collapse in Game Six as Denkinger was. The magazine also deplored the poor sportsmanship of the Cardinals in Game Seven in a sidebar story which labeled the Cards "the nuthouse gang."

Many fans refused to buy it, though. To them the 1985 World Series would always be the one Don Denkinger cost them, despite St. Louis' pitiful .185 batting average for the Series, despite the fact that the Cardinals could score only 13 runs in seven games. One bitter letter to *Sports Illustrated* was typical of the frustration of Cardinals fans. It said, in part, "The Cardinals were only three outs from winning the Series. It took them 108 victories to get into that position, and an umpire who didn't do anything to get there took it away from them. No big deal, just another bad call. Sure."

It was a bad call. Denkinger himself admitted it after viewing replays. It was no worse than other bad calls. Unfortunately for Denkinger, it just happened to come at the worst possible time. And St. Louis Cardinals fans will never allow him to forget it.

Chapter 24

Wrestled Off the Bag: Drew Coble's Out Call (1991 World Series)

Before 1991, if a poll of baseball historians had been taken to determine which of the 87 previous World Series had been the greatest, three years would probably have scored highest. The wonderful seven games played between the Boston Red Sox and the Cincinnati Reds in 1975 would rate near the top. Five of the games were decided by just one run. Two of them required extra innings, including Game Six, famous for Carlton Fisk's twelfth-inning drive over Fenway Park's left-field wall, the "Green Monster." Older fans might have selected the 1947 World Series as the best ever played. That was the autumn when New York's Bill Bevens took a no-hitter into the ninth inning, only to have Cookie Lavagetto hit a two-out double which not only spoiled Bevens' bid for immortality but also drove in the tying and winning runs for Brooklyn. The 1947 World Series is also famous for Al Gionfriddo's desperate lunging catch in Game Six which deprived Joe DiMaggio of an extra-base hit, saving the day for the Dodgers. Some diligent historians maintain that the 1912 World Series may have been the best ever. Why? For one reason, it took eight games to play a best-of-seven Series! Game Two, called on account of darkness, ended in a 6–6 tie, and eventually an eighth game was needed to break the deadlock between the Red Sox and the New York Giants. The conclusion of Game

Eight was wild. With the game tied after nine innings, the Giants scored once in the top of the tenth, but Boston notched two in the chaotic home half to win the game and the Series.

After 1991, some perspectives were altered. Minnesota edged Atlanta in seven games in a World Series which featured so many nail-biters that some grizzled reporters were forced to admit that the 1991 Series must be considered among the greatest the sport has ever seen. True, the Minnesota Twins and Atlanta Braves were not, for the most part, glamorous franchises, which may diminish the Series' significance in the eyes of those who remember the 1947 Dodgers-Yankees affair. However, for dramatics and sheer enjoyment, the 1991 World Series has few rivals in history. Making it even more remarkable was the fact that both Atlanta and Minnesota had finished at the bottom of the standings the previous season.

In 1990, scalpers were having trouble giving away tickets to Atlanta Braves' home games. Few fans bothered to spend their money to watch a club that won just 65 of 162 games. Atlanta finished the 1990 season in the basement, 26 games behind frontrunning Cincinnati. In fact, the Braves were so weak that they were ten full games behind the next worst team in the NL West, the San Diego Padres. The Minnesota Twins also had it rough in 1990. Although they were statistically better than Atlanta, winning 74 games, they were buried in the AL West, 29 games behind pennant-winning Oakland. At the end of the 1990 season, the mere thought of a Minnesota-Atlanta World Series in 1991 was utterly ludicrous.

Much to the amazement of baseball fans, both the Twins and the Braves staged improbable turnarounds in 1991. Aided by the timely hitting of National League batting champion Terry Pendleton and the capable arm of 20-game winner Tom Glavine, the Braves managed to capture the NL West title in 1991 by a slim one-game margin over the Los Angeles Dodgers. The Twins, by comparison, had it easy, winning the AL West by an eight-game margin over Chicago. Minnesota did not boast any AL leaders in offensive categories, but relied on a sturdy pitching staff featuring Scott Erickson (winner of 20 games), Jack Morris (18 wins), and Kevin Tapani (16 wins). Minnesota stunned the favored Toronto Blue Jays in the American League Championship Series, ousting Toronto in five games, even winning the last three at SkyDome. Atlanta, however, had a more difficult playoff route. After five games of the NLCS, the Pittsburgh Pirates led the Braves three games to two, with the series heading back to Pittsburgh. But Atlanta's pitching stunned the Pittsburgh fans and saved the day with two consecutive shutouts, as Atlanta earned the right to meet Minnesota in a World Series pairing 1990 doormats.

The 1991 World Series was not only a battle between the Twins and the Braves but also a clash of hokey gimmicks spawned by the teams' fans. In Atlanta, the Braves' fans had borrowed the "tomahawk chop" cheer from Florida State University. Within a short time, every Atlanta fan, from the youngest urchin to Jane Fonda, was chopping rhythmically to war-dance music from Fulton County Stadium's public address system. At the Metrodome, the fans, who had also stayed away in droves in 1990, were now gleefully waving "homer hankies" to inspire their beloved Twins. As fans arrived at Minnesota's home park for Game One of the World Series, they were met by a peculiar sight. A group of politically correct zealots were demonstrating against the "tomahawk chop" and the Braves' team nickname. Claiming them to be insulting to the heritage of Native Americans, the picketers attempted to persuade fans not to enter the stadium. Needless to say, the protesters experienced little success. In fact, the demonstration produced several incidents of racial insults and scuffles. Apparently, many Minnesota fans wanted to attend a major sporting event to escape the petty disagreements which were becoming a part of daily society, not to participate in such a debate.

With the protesters' leaflets going largely unread, Game One began with Jack Morris starting on the mound for Minnesota and Charlie Leibrandt doing the honors for Atlanta. Morris' seven solid innings earned him the victory, but it was the long-ball hitting of the Twins that really mattered in Game One. Greg Gagne's three-run homer in the fifth inning, followed by a solo home run by Kent Hrbek in the sixth, broke the game open and powered the Twins to a 5–2 win. The next night, October 20, Hrbek would demonstrate his strength again, but in a highly controversial manner.

Kent Hrbek is a huge physical specimen. Weighing 257 pounds, the muscular Minnesota first baseman acquired his physique by engaging in an extensive weight-training program. Hrbek is also a big fan of the professional wrestling circuit, and plans to become one of the grappling thespians when his baseball career ends. A common sight in the Twins locker room before each game is Hrbek walking around in a T-shirt which says "T-Rex." That, according to Hrbek, is the ring name he has chosen for himself in his next career. In a critical moment of Game Two, it appeared that Hrbek was getting in a little wrestling practice while playing first base, much to the dismay of the Atlanta Braves and Ron Gant, their diminutive outfielder.

Tom Glavine started Game Two for the Braves and immediately got himself in trouble by allowing a two-run homer to Chili Davis in the bottom of the first inning. Atlanta struck back with one run in the top of the second inning off the Twins' starter, Kevin Tapani. The score stayed at 2–1 entering the top of the third. With one out, Atlanta's Lonnie Smith reached first base on Scott Leius' error. One out later, Ron Gant connected for a single to left field. Dan Gladden, the Minnesota left fielder, picked up the ball and threw to third base. His throw, however, was off the mark and eluded third baseman Leius. Fortunately for the Twins, pitcher Kevin Tapani was backing up the play. Tapani gloved the ball as it rolled past Leius, preventing Smith from scoring. Tapani then eyed Gant, who had rounded first base. Hoping to catch Gant napping, Tapani fired the ball to Kent Hrbek, who was stationed at first. Gant retreated to the bag and easily beat Hrbek's tag. However, as Jim Donaghy of the Associated Press described the situation, "the 170-pound Gant and the 250-pound Hrbek ended up in a twist of arms and legs." Using the full force of his bulk, Hrbek appeared to lift Gant off the bag. Hrbek applied another tag, and to the amazement of Gant, first base coach Pat Corrales, and millions of television viewers, umpire Drew Coble declared Gant out.

Immediately, an incensed Gant confronted Coble. Shouting that Hrbek had illegally pulled him off the bag, Gant berated Coble until he was pulled away by coach Corrales. In the CBS broadcast booth, special guest announcer Tommy Lasorda referred to Coble's decision as "a terrible call." Donaghy's report on the game agreed with Lasorda's assessment. "TV replays seem to show Hrbek, a pro wrestling fan, lifting Gant off the base in a move Hulk Hogan would be proud of," wrote Donaghy. "It was the third out and spared Tapani the problem of facing Dave Justice with runners on first and third."

After the game, a distraught Gant gave the media his version of what happened. *Sports Illustrated* quoted: "I was definitely on the base. . . . I'm sure everyone watching on television and in the stadium knew I was on the base. Since when can you just pull a guy off the base?" Naturally, Hrbek had a different point of view. "His momentum carried him into me," Hrbek said of Gant. "I kept my glove on his leg. I knew he was going to fall off the base because his momentum was carrying him off." When Gant was told that Hrbek felt he had slipped off the base, Gant refuted Hrbek's claim. "I felt the whole force of him pulling me off the bag. He's twice my size."

The end of Atlanta's rally in the third inning may have cost the Braves the game. Although Atlanta tied the score in the top of the fifth inning, Minnesota third baseman Scott Leius redeemed his earlier error by hitting a solo home run off Glavine. It proved to be the difference, as Minnesota won Game Two by a score of 3–2. The Twins now held a two-games-to-none lead, heading for Atlanta. Leius' game-winning home run should have been the major topic of discussion in postgame interviews, but the Hrbek-Gant tangle at first base in the third inning was more noteworthy. Rule-book aficionados stated that while there is nothing in the laws of the game which states a runner can't be yanked off a base, there is nothing that permits it either. It has become standard practice to deny any out made by a fielder who has clearly and deliberately knocked a runner from his acquired base. As one columnist pointed out, there is nothing written in the rule book saying that you can't hit a runner over the head with a tire iron, but common sense says it should not be allowed.

The debate continued through the next day, a Monday, while the clubs traveled to Georgia. When asked by reporters if he had been getting in some wrestling practice on the play, Hrbek replied,

"No. T-Rex has a few more baseball games to play first." CBS milked the controversy for all it was worth. They summoned American League umpire Don Denkinger for his opinion about the play. Denkinger, keeping with the tradition which forbids an umpire from publicly criticizing a colleague, agreed with Coble's decision, stating that Gant's momentum had caused him to break contact with the base. Denkinger's support of Coble was ironic to those who remembered Denkinger as the umpire in the 1985 World Series who made one of the most famous and costly officiating blunders in baseball history (see chapter 23). Adding a little levity to the situation, CBS, in its pregame show before Game Three, invited popular professional wrestler Randy "Macho Man" Savage to "analyze" Hrbek's "takedown" in his inimitable style. By this point, every baseball fan in North America was convinced Hrbek's tag on Gant had been illegal.

With every reason to be discouraged by their two losses in Minnesota, the Braves returned home to their tomahawk-chopping fans for the next three games, and surprised many observers by winning them all. The Braves won Game Three, on October 22, in a 12-inning marathon, 5–4, when Mark Lemke drove home David Justice with the decisive run. Lemke was the hero again the following evening. With the score tied 2–2 in the bottom of the ninth, Lemke tripled and later scored on a sacrifice fly by pinch-hitter Jerry Willard. The pivotal Game Five also went to Atlanta, but this time the game was a rout. The Braves won by a 14–5 score. Dave Justice, Lonnie Smith, and Brian Hunter all hit home runs in the lopsided affair. Atlanta's 14 runs were the most scored by one team in a World Series game since 1960. More important was the fact that the Braves had taken control of the Series and now led three games to two, heading back to Minneapolis.

Game Six was the heartbreaker for Atlanta. The Twins won the game in 11 innings, 4–3, when superstar outfielder Kirby Puckett hit a game-winning blast off Charlie Leibrandt. Game Seven was a pitching masterpiece which also was not decided until more than nine innings had been played. Minnesota's Jack Morris did not allow a Braves run through nine innings. Atlanta used three hurlers, John Smoltz, Mike Stanton, and Alejandro Peña, but also managed to keep Minnesota off the scoreboard through nine innings. Morris kept his shutout through the tenth inning, but Peña faltered. With the bases loaded, Gene Larkin lofted a single into center field to win the game for Minnesota, 1–0. The victory sealed the 1991 World Series for the Twins in seven games. For just the second time in World Series history, each game had been won by the home team. Oddly enough, the Minnesota Twins were involved on both occasions, knocking off the St. Louis Cardinals in 1987 and then the Atlanta Braves four years later. In their three World Series appearances, the Minnesota Twins have posted a remarkable home record of 11 wins and just one loss. The lone loss, coming in Game Seven of the 1965 World Series, was excusable. Sandy Koufax, at the height of his powers, defeated the Twins 2–0 in Game Seven to win the World Series for the Los Angeles Dodgers.

Atlanta fans were still proud of their team in defeat. The resurrection of the Braves from patsies to National League champions had been completed within the space of 12 months. The Braves had come within one run of claiming the world championship. This was indeed a feat worth applauding. But what if Drew Coble had not called Gant out on the tag play in the third inning of Game Two? Couldn't that have made a world of difference? The bad call and its end results are realities which Atlanta fans will have to, um, wrestle with for years to come.

Chapter 25

The Triple Play That Wasn't, and Other Gaffes of the 1992 World Series

In the history of the World Series, there has only been one triple play—at least, only one that counted—and it was spectacular. The momentous event occurred on the afternoon of October 10, 1920, during Game Five of that year's World Series. The visiting Brooklyn Dodgers were trailing the Cleveland Indians 7–0 in the top of the fifth inning when Brooklyn started to rally. Pete Kilduff led off with a single. Otto Miller followed with another single, sending Kilduff to second. The next batter was Clarence Mitchell, Brooklyn's pitcher, but a decent hitter for his position. Mitchell connected for a line drive off Indian pitcher Jim Bagby. Both runners took off, as the ball appeared to be headed for the gap in right-center field.

Bill Wambsganss, Cleveland's second baseman, darted to his right and caught the ball on the fly before it even got to the outfield. Mitchell was out. Immediately, Wambsganss stepped on second base to retire Kilduff, who was still running toward third. Also still running was Miller, unaware of Wambsganss' catch. Without having to move very far, Wambsganss tagged Miller for the third out. Cleveland had turned a triple play. More accurately, Wambsganss had turned an unassisted triple play, the rarest of all defensive gems. There had never been a triple play in World Series competition before Wambsganss' feat, and there has not been one since.

Well, actually there has been. Millions of television viewers tuned to the 1992 World Series saw one. The problem was that umpire Bob Davidson missed a tag which Toronto's Kelly Gruber applied to the foot of Deion Sanders. Had Davidson not erred on the play, the Blue Jays would have turned a triple play of their own which would have rivaled the jewel recorded by Bill Wambsganss back in 1920.

The triple play controversy was just one of three hot topics which surfaced during the 1992 World Series. Two of them, including Bob Davidson's mistake, focused on erroneous calls made by the split officiating crew assigned to work the Toronto-Atlanta series. The third incident had nothing to do with baseball; it was a comical, unbelievable faux pas in international protocol which had Canadian baseball fans fuming and eventually produced apologies from major league baseball officials and President George Bush.

When Toronto knocked off Oakland in the 1992 American League Championship Series, two milestones were achieved. First, the Blue Jays had finally overcome the hurdle which had seemed to loom higher than Mount Everest. Three times in the previous seven seasons the Blue Jays had won the AL East title only to lose to the AL West champions. In 1985, the Kansas City Royals had rallied to dump Toronto. In 1989, Oakland had ended the Jays' quest for a World Series berth. Minnesota had stunned the Blue Jays in 1991. The word was out: Toronto can't win the big games. The 1992 ALCS dispelled that notion. The Blue Jays vanquished the powerful Oakland A's in six games.

Now, for the first time ever, the World Series would be played in a stadium beyond the American border. Toronto's opponents would be the Atlanta Braves, who had miraculously rallied in Game Seven of the NLCS, scoring three runs in the bottom of the ninth inning to upend Pittsburgh.

With a Canadian-based team playing in one of America's great sporting events, it was only natural that some sort of international incident would occur. Canadians, by nature, are insecure about their cultural identity, having been overwhelmed by American influence in its numerous outlets. Among the most sensitive issues for Canadians is the woeful lack of knowledge most Americans seem to have about their northern neighbors. Stories circulate about naïve American tourists who enter Canada in July hoping for a wonderful holiday of skiing. Others, so the stories go, fully expect to visit Queen Elizabeth in Ottawa or see moose and caribou grazing in downtown Toronto. Some members of the Atlanta Braves did little to diminish this concept of American ignorance when they declared they probably wouldn't travel around much in Toronto because of the French language problems they were sure to encounter. Allison Gordon, one of Canada's top sports journalists, was quick to inform the Braves that Toronto's francophone population is tiny, but that one might run into a lot of Italian- or Portuguese-speaking Torontonians. It all made for hearty laughs in the Canadian newspapers, until the unthinkable happened before Game Two of the World Series in Atlanta: the U.S. Marine color guard paraded onto the field for the national anthems with the Canadian flag displayed upside down!

Canadian television viewers—and there were millions of them—were aghast. Emotions ranged from amusement to disbelief to anger. The switchboard at CTV, the Canadian network which was picking up the CBS feed, was "beyond swamped" with phone calls, according to news reports. Photographs of the improperly flying flag appeared on the front page of virtually every Canadian newspaper the next morning. Even though it was an obvious mistake, some hypersensitive Canadians believed that the marines had deliberately "desecrated" one of Canada's national symbols. Steve Rushin of *Sports Illustrated* noted that while baseball officials claimed the flag debacle was wholly unintentional, "others suspected it was intentionally unholy."

"We feel pretty bad," stated Sgt. Sandy Wilson of the marines. "Some young marine was handed a flag and put it up in haste. He might not have ever seen that flag before." That explanation did not satisfy a lot of Canadians, including a reporter for *Globe and Mail* who commented, "Atlanta is supposed to be a world-class city capable of hosting the Olympics. If they can't get the Canadian flag right, imagine what might happen to the Kenyans and Albanians in 1996." Those in charge of the World Series were embarrassed, and promptly issued a formal apology, which was read over the air by CBS' Sean McDonough during the second inning:

> Major league baseball apologizes to the people of Canada and to all baseball fans for the unintentional improper display of the Canadian flag during the national anthems prior to the start of tonight's World Series game.

President Bush also issued an apology from the White House. The marines humbly asked for a second chance to have the "privilege" of carrying the Canadian flag in Toronto before Game Three. It was granted and this time there was no mix-up.

However, before Game Two was half over, a second controversy flared up. With Atlanta leading 1–0 in the top of the fourth inning, Toronto's Roberto Alomar was standing on third base representing the tying run. When pitcher John Smoltz unleashed a pitch which eluded catcher Damon Berryhill, Alomar broke for the plate. Berryhill retrieved the ball and threw to Smoltz, who had come in from the mound to cover home. Alomar's head-first slide was clearly under Smoltz's late tag. Nevertheless, plate umpire Mike Reilly emphatically called Alomar out. Long, emotional protestations by Alomar and Toronto manager Cito Gaston proved fruitless, and Reilly's bad call remained unchanged. If it had not been for a late Toronto rally, which enabled the Blue Jays to win the game 5–4, Reilly's decision would have generated more irate phone calls to Canada's open-line radio shows than the color guard's blunder.

The next game would feature the triple play that wasn't. Toronto and Atlanta were level at one game apiece. Game Three would be the first World Series game contested outside the United States. Enterprising vendors were peddling T-shirts emblazoned with upside-down American flags above the caption, "Sorry, eh!" A group of Blue Jay fans attempted to hang a banner from the SkyDome's upper deck which said, "No hard feelings"—displayed upside down, of course. Some humorless security staff at the stadium seized the banner.

With the game scoreless in the top of the fourth inning, Atlanta had the makings of a rally. Deion Sanders, the Braves' outlandish part-time outfielder, was on second base. Terry Pendleton was on first. Nobody was out when David Justice lashed a drive to deep center field off Toronto ace Jimmy Key. Center fielder Devon White, one of the game's best defensive outfielders, sensed the ball was heading for the wall, took his eye off the ball, and charged toward the padded barrier. As he approached the fence, White found the ball in his sights once again, jumped, made a backhanded grab, and thudded chest-first into the padding.

It was a sensational play, but it was only the beginning. Sanders had run more than halfway to third and was now retreating to second. Pendleton had already rounded second, convinced that White was not going to catch Justice's drive. Sanders passed Pendleton on his way back to second. Pendleton was now ahead of Sanders on the basepath, which meant that Pendleton was automatically out. As White relayed the ball to the infield, several umpires were signalling that Pendleton had been declared out and no play was necessary to retire him. But the cutoff man, not realizing that Pendleton no longer mattered, threw the ball to first baseman John Olerud, who stepped on the bag. Sensing that a triple play could be made, Olerud fired the ball to third baseman Kelly Gruber. Sanders had retouched second base during the confusion and was now recklessly trying to advance to third. When Gruber received the ball, Sanders was caught in a rundown and looked certain to be the third out on a spectacular triple play. Gruber charged at the swift but rattled Sanders. As Sanders attempted to dive back to second, Gruber lunged at him and clearly tagged his left foot while Sanders was five feet from the bag. Sanders sprawled back to the base believing he was out. Gruber knew he had tagged Sanders. So did all the television viewers. Amazingly, umpire Bob Davidson, who was right on top of the play, ruled that Gruber had missed Sanders with the tag and called him safe.

Out of the Toronto dugout came Cito Gaston again, perplexed at the second consecutive bad call the Jays had gotten on what appeared to be obvious mistakes. Gruber pleaded that he had tagged Sanders. The arguments were to no avail, of course, and the game continued. Another late Toronto rally enabled the Jays to win 3–2 and take a two-games-to-one lead in the World Series. That was fine with the Blue Jays and their fans, but Bob Davidson's call had denied them a piece of history.

"I hit him [Sanders] on the back of the heel," Gruber said in a *Sports Illustrated* story, referring to the tag play. Television replays conclusively proved that Gruber was right and umpire Davidson was wrong. Later, when shown the replay from various angles, Davidson was honest enough to say, "I thought I was correct at first, but then I saw the pictures, and I had to admit I probably missed it." Bill Wambsganss and the 1920 Cleveland Indians were still recognized as the only triple-play-makers in World Series history, even though the honor should be shared with the 1992 Toronto Blue Jays.

With momentum clearly on their side, Toronto won Game Four 2–1 on Devon White's RBI single in the eighth inning. Poised to win the World Series at home in Game Five, the Blue Jays were rocked 7–2. Atlanta scored five runs in the fifth inning, the key hit being Lonnie Smith's grand slam homer off Toronto starter Jack Morris. The two clubs packed their belongings and headed back to Atlanta for Game Six. In a memorable contest, Toronto managed to win 4–3 in 11 innings. Atlanta had battled back to tie the game 2–2 in the ninth, and were on the verge of erasing a two-run Blue Jay cushion in the eleventh. Atlanta's hopes of a World Series championship ended when Otis Nixon was thrown out at first by reliever Mike Timlin on an attempted bunt play. As the delirious Blue Jays celebrated on the field in Atlanta, thousands of Toronto fans whooped it up 700 miles away. Many of them were watching the game on the Jumbotron in the SkyDome. When the final out was made, hundreds descended onto the field to celebrate, no doubt trying to embrace players who were not there.

The Series was now history and the Blue Jays were world champions, but many were still dissatisfied with the glaring errors of the umpiring crew during the six games. In a sidebar story titled "The Men of Blew," *Sports Illustrated* addressed the issue. "Two years ago baseball stopped assigning umpires for postseason play on a rotation basis—a scheme that ensured that if you were an ump and breathing, you'd get to work a World Series—and went to a merit system." The story went on to explain that it was not a true merit system. A pool of umpires deemed to have done well during the regular season was made available by the directors of umpiring for both major leagues. The directors then chose those from the pool who were due to work a World Series. "In other words," the article pointed out, "any halfway decent umpire who hasn't done a Series recently could still get picked."

The article continued, "As the umpiring in this year's Series showed, the new system isn't much better than the old one. Of the six umps selected, three were working their first Series, three had one Series under their belts, and none were crew chiefs. Some of the umpires were very good, but some is not enough. The best teams in baseball deserve the best umpires, even if it means some of the same guys popping up every year."

The writer of the article, Bruce Newman, raised some good points. The World Series is baseball's showcase event, and the best umpires should be there every year, regardless of how many times they have been there before. Bill Klem, a National League umpire whose career spanned 36 years, from 1906 to 1941, appeared in 18 different World Series, including five straight from 1911 to 1915. Why? Because he was one of the best men in blue in his day. There was no outcry among the teams when Klem became a regular fixture in the World Series, because everyone knew that quality was not being sacrificed with Klem on the diamond. The 1992 World Series should have sent the message that a rotation system, no matter how it is disguised, should not be more important than quality. Mike Reilly and Bob Davidson proved that conclusively.

Epilogue

Third Strike: The Aborted 1994 Season

> I think that a union sounds like a very good thing. But don't get me wrong. I don't think ball players should or ever would strike. We love the game too much.
>
> —Eddie Mathews of the Milwaukee Braves, quoted in *Sports Illustrated* in 1957

When the 1994 baseball season began, a fresh wind of optimism was blowing through the major leagues. Brand-new parks with old-fashioned ambience opened their gates in Cleveland and Arlington, injecting vigor into dormant franchises. Projections for overall attendance records were made. Cal Ripken, Jr., was within sight of Lou Gehrig's seemingly untouchable record of 2,130 consecutive games played. Although many of the sport's purists cringed at the majors' new six-division alignment, which allowed second-place clubs into the post-season for the first time in a century, others rejoiced at the rejuvenation of the great Yankee and Dodger franchises, which had slumped badly in the early 1990s. Fans also thrilled at the prospect of legitimate individual assaults on the .400 batting average and the 61-home-run mark.... And then it was gone. In an unprecedented move, major-league baseball abruptly ceased operations because of yet another labor dispute. It was a miserable way to celebrate the 125th anniversary of professional baseball.

Beginning in the early 1970s, the sports section of any major daily newspaper could easily be confused with the business pages. Strikes, arbitrators, negotiators, lockouts, walkouts, holdouts, contracts, reserve clauses, and free agency became terms that baseball fans were beginning to understand, but not necessarily like. For nearly 100 years, those who closely followed the action on the field had been mercifully spared the dealings which took place in boardrooms and conference centers. The club owners, almost from day one, had cornered the market on player talent with an ingenious legal device called the reserve clause.

The reserve clause was originally established to prevent rival big-league clubs from acquiring the services of other clubs' star players. The way it worked was the essence of simplicity. When a player signed a contract with a major-league club, he was putting his name to a document which contained a section binding him to that team—even after the contract expired when the season ended. Originally, only marquee players were bound to their original clubs by the reserve clause. (In fact, many nineteenth-century stars took it as a compliment to be "reserved." It meant that they had virtual guarantees for jobs the following season.) Soon, however, every major-league contract had the perpetual reserve clause added to it. Major-league baseball players, unlike ordinary American citizens, could not move freely from employer to employer. Players changed teams only if they were traded to or purchased by another club. The result was obvious: a player either re-signed with the club which owned his rights, at whatever salary was being offered, or gave up professional baseball altogether.

The lone negotiating tool that players had was to threaten to hold out until their individual contract demands were met. Babe Ruth almost always returned his contract to the Yankees unsigned. Only after his demands were satisfied did Ruth agree to put on his uniform for another season. Of course, Ruth had the unique attribute of being the most famous athlete in America and baseball's foremost drawing card, so he had greater negotiating clout than any of his contemporaries. Still, it was not uncommon for lesser lights to threaten to quit the sport and begin another vocation rather than accept the measly terms offered by owners. Dale Mitchell, most widely known for being the final batter retired in Don Larsen's perfect game, set a record for perseverance by holding out for seven years! Still, the negotiating power clearly belonged to the owners.

The reserve clause was as much a part of baseball as the seventh-inning stretch, until 1969. That year, Curt Flood of the St. Louis Cardinals was traded against his wishes to the Philadelphia Phillies. Flood had spent 12 productive seasons in St. Louis and had established business and family ties in that city. Nearing the end of his career, and not wanting to uproot his life and move to Philadelphia, Flood balked at the trade. He refused to report to the Phillies, claiming that he was a human being and not chattel. "I do not feel I am a piece of property to be bought and sold irrespective of my wishes," Flood wrote to Commissioner Bowie Kuhn. Claiming that the reserve clause smacked of indentured servitude, if not slavery, Flood took his case all the way to the U.S. Supreme Court, but lost a 5–3 decision. The baseball establishment was relieved, but the closeness of the verdict and the hint that it might be reversed in other cases worried the owners. Outright free agency, under which players could move from team to team after each season, would kill the game, they claimed. Wouldn't the wealthy teams simply pluck the best players from the poorer clubs?

The once rock-solid reserve clause now was on wobbly legs. The final blow came late in 1975. Pitchers Dave McNally and Andy Messersmith became "test cases" after they opted to play the 1975 season without signing contracts. As was customary, they received their 1974 salaries. Once the 1975 campaign had concluded, both men declared themselves free agents, maintaining that their playing without contracts for 12 months had freed them from the dreaded clutches of the reserve clause. Arbitrator Peter Seitz agreed that the two pitchers had "played out their option" and were free to sign with any team they chose. For all intents and purposes, the reserve clause was dead.

The predictable economic activity took place. Free agents now went to the highest bidder. In the ensuing frenzy of activity, salaries rose dramatically. During the 1968 season, the average major-league salary was a laughably low $19,000. By 1983 it had risen to approximately $300,000. Fans were appalled that players of ordinary talent were now demanding and receiving six-figure contracts. They were further galled by the dramatic rise in ticket prices, concession food, and all the other miscellaneous expenses that come with attending a ball game. Traditionalists mourned the lack of continuity from year to year on team rosters. With easy money to be made by jumping from team to team, would there ever again be the likes of Bob Feller, Ted Williams, or Joe DiMaggio—men whose entire careers had been spent with one club? Others were glad that tightfisted owners of an earlier era, such as Connie Mack and Calvin Griffith, were no longer around to see what the demise of the reserve clause had wrought.

Thanks to multimillion-dollar television pacts, the owners were free to shower even greater riches on their players by the late 1980s. When baseball wages began to pass the million-dollar mark, Tony Kubek, the shortstop of the fabulous 1961 Yankees, was asked his opinion about the spiralling salaries. "The only thing more ridiculous than the salaries paid during the free agent era," Kubek said, "were the salaries we were paid before free agency." As evidence, Kubek noted that Hank Aaron earned just $44,000 in 1974, the year he smashed Babe Ruth's career home-run record.

The owners, who were crying poverty even though their franchises' wealth had grown considerably, tried to regain some measure of economic control. The 50-day strike which disrupted the 1981 season and the one-day walkout of 1985 were largely due to the players balking at the fiscal reform the owners deemed necessary. In 1987 the owners attempted another tactic. They simply refused to sign any free agents. Superstars such as Andre Dawson and Jack Morris were, amazingly, not sought by any club. "Collusion!" cried the players' union. And collusion it was, according to the law. The owners were forced to cough up nearly $300 million in fines and penalties.

Salaries in the 1990s grew beyond the wildest expectations of Andy Messersmith. The nightly news reported player signings of $3 million, $4 million, and $5 million per year. When Barry Bonds signed a multi-year contract which paid him more than $42 million over six seasons, mathematicians dutifully calculated that the terms of the deal could pay the salary of the President of the United States for more than 200 years. The fans, who had tended to sympathize with the players in the labor disputes through 1981, began to sour. Players, in many fans' opinions, had become more interested in their investment portfolios than in their batting averages. They had also become more and more detached from the paying public. Autographs, in many instances, often came at a price. For many families, the simple pleasure of attending a major-league game was no longer affordable. When the 1994 season began, the average salary in the big leagues was close to $1.2 million. The beloved national pastime had been transformed into big business in the course of two turbulent decades.

Trouble was brewing before the 1994 season ever began. No agreement had been reached between players' union and the owners. Nevertheless, Opening Day came on schedule. Two new picturesque parks—Jacobs Field in Cleveland and The Ballpark in Arlington, Texas, with modern conveniences but the old-fashioned look, similar to Baltimore's Oriole Park at Camden Yards—saw their first big-league action. The new homes of the Cleveland Indians and Texas Rangers immediately won rave reviews for the distinctive baseball atmosphere they exuded. Fans began to count down the games separating Cal Ripken, Jr., and the immortal Lou Gehrig's fabulous record. From a distance, baseball looked healthier than ever.

But the trappings were just an illusion. The owners, tired of escalating player salaries, were determined to institute some type of limit—a salary cap—on how much teams could pay their players. Small-market cities such as San Diego, Milwaukee, and Seattle were often used as examples of teams that were in imminent danger of financial ruin if operating costs were not contained. The National Basketball Association had implemented a salary cap when many of its franchises were in dire straits, baseball's owners were quick to point out, and not long afterward the NBA was flourishing. As of 1994, National Football League teams were similarly limiting their payrolls. But major-league baseball players were having none of it. A salary cap would artificially restrict every player's true market value, they said.

The first four months of the 1994 season generated excitement in a number of areas. Matt Williams and Ken Griffey, Jr., were launching balls over fences at record rates. Frank Thomas of the White Sox had a legitimate shot at being the first Triple Crown winner since 1967. Unheralded Paul O'Neill of the Yankees flirted with a .400 batting average for three months, but faded. Almost on cue, San Diego's Tony Gwynn began his run at it. Even the major-league records for doubles and RBIs in a season, both set during the hit-happy 1930s, were in danger of falling. Montreal, Cleveland, and Texas joined Los Angeles and the Yankees as rejuvenated clubs on their way to the post-season. Then the economic realities of 1990s baseball set in.

The players' union, dismayed by the lack of progress in its negotiations with the owners, established an August 12 strike date. Sporadic meetings settled nothing. The owners were adamant that a salary cap of some sort was essential for the survival of many teams. The players refused to budge an inch on this matter. Such a limitation on their earnings was unpalatable, but they claimed that freedom was the issue, not money. When the August 12 games concluded with no progress achieved in the boardrooms, the strike—the third mid-season interruption since 1981—was on.

The reaction of baseball fans was noticeably different in 1994 than it had been in 1981. The 50-day work stoppage in 1981 was received with incredulity. No baseball on the Fourth of July? How peculiar! Strikes had affected and disrupted virtually all facets of American life at one time or another. Why not the national pastime? In 1994, a greater sense of anger encompassed the followers of the game. More and more people found it difficult to comprehend why millionaire athletes considered themselves oppressed. In one of the final games before the strike, a placard at one major-league stadium said, "I'll play for $100,000. I'll provide my own uniform and equipment. It'll be a sacrifice, but I think I can handle it."

Although the owners were also targets of the fans' displeasure—they were accused of being tightwads who weren't willing to fairly share baseball's vast varieties of revenues—the players took the brunt of the heat. Letters written by disillusioned fans to *Sports Illustrated* were indicative of the nation's collective disgust. Some vowed to boycott the sport if and when it returned. "This is one fan who will not be back," wrote a man from Alabama. "Wake up, Boys of Summer. You need us but we don't need you." A common gripe was over the exorbitant salaries already paid to the striking players. An Ohioan commented, "I'm hard-pressed to feel sorry for guys making $1.2 million a year for playing a game that allows them to take 15 or 30 days off when they hit a padded wall or step too hard on a bag, to renegotiate a contract when they think they have done well and to get a bonus for doing what they were paid to do in the first place." The whole idea of baseball players needing a union rankled a reader from Los Angeles. "Long live organized labor," he wrote sarcastically. "It's time that the players were freed from the yokes that bind them to multimillion-dollar contracts, eight-month work years, mansions and Mercedes."

After a few days of hopeless negotiating, the impasse remained. As the strike dragged on into September, there was still little hope on the horizon for a resolution which would save the scintillating 1994 baseball campaign. Some cynics claimed that the owners were deliberately sabotaging the talks to achieve their hidden agenda—the cancellation of the season and the destruction of the players' union. Other observers suggested that clubs suffering through dismal seasons (such as Toronto, Boston, and Detroit) were so far out of the divisional races that their owners had little to gain by resuming the season. The bickering and accusations continued until the afternoon of September 16, when acting commissioner Bud Selig made an historic annoucement from Milwaukee. He somberly informed the assembled media that the owners had overwhelmingly voted to cancel the remainder of the 1994 season. For the first time since 1904, no World Series would be played.

Reactions to the announcement ranged from apathy to disbelief. Predictably, the fans whose teams were in contention for a playoff spot were most upset. Others simply shrugged and accepted the inconvenience. "No more baseball! That's a shame, but when do the Dallas Cowboys play this weekend?" Neither side in the dispute could take any comfort in how Selig's announcement had failed to affect the average American sports fan. There were no riots or suicides because the baseball season had ended abruptly in mid–August. After a couple of days, fans who normally divided their attention in September between the pennant races and football simply concentrated wholly on gridiron action. It was stunningly apparent that major-league baseball was no longer as important to the American public as it had been to previous generations.

Who was to blame for the indifference of the fans? The players? Certainly. Their salaries, exorbitant by any standard, had alienated them from the public. For much of baseball's history, most players earned little more than those who bought tickets to watch them. This had all changed after the legal victory achieved by McNally and Messersmith. Free agency had turned the players into mercenaries, denying fans the pleasant tradition of watching them toil for the same clubs from season to season. If players could abandon team loyalty for the almighty buck, who could blame the fans for losing interest?

The owners must also accept their share of fault, too. No one ever forced an owner at gunpoint to make an enormous offer to a ballplayer. Perhaps if the owners had been more generous with contracts during the era of the reserve clause, the players might not be as militant and cantankerous in the 1990s.

Of course, the hapless victims of baseball's becoming big business are the fans. They are often taken for granted. Raise the ticket prices year after year, and they still come back. Break up championship teams, and they still come back. Throw tradition out the window by elminating true pennant races, and they still come back. Disrupt a season with a strike, and they still come back. This time, though, some have vowed not to come back. Even "fan unions" have sprung up here and there as a way for the general public to express disgust with the contemporary sports scene, but their effectiveness has been minimal at best. Few fans, for whatever the reason, have the fortitude to boycott the sport they love regardless of the injuries that have been inflicted on them. Legendary Detroit broadcaster Ernie Harwell has likened the average baseball fan to a spouse in an abusive marriage: no matter how much punishment and neglect is dished out, the victim meekly returns for more.

Major-league baseball has been blessed throughout its history with an unrivalled ability to win its fans back. Some observers thought the stain from the fixed 1919 World Series would permanently damage the sport, but Babe Ruth's booming bat restored interest. The Great Depression of the 1930s took its toll on attendance, but the novelty of night games provided the remedy. Often it has taken years for major-league baseball to truly regain its health. But it is a resilient institution. If the sport can endure scandals, depressions, and wars, it will likely survive this present down period as well. The damage done by the 1994 strike is significant, but probably not fatal.

Bibliography

Angell, Roger. *Late Innings*. New York, NY: Random House, 1982.

Asinof, Eliot. *Eight Men Out*. New York, NY: Ace, 1963.

Flood, Curt. *The Way It Is*. Richmond Hill, Ontario: Pocket Books, 1971.

Flynn, George L. *Great Moments in Baseball*. Hong Kong: Bison Books, 1987.

Gropman, Donald. *Say It Ain't So, Joe!* New York, NY: Lynx Books, 1988.

Halberstrom, David. *The Summer of '49*. New York, NY: William Morrow, 1989.

Honig, Donald. *Baseball America*. New York, NY: Macmillan, 1985.

Major League Baseball (production). *Make the Right Call*. Chicago: Triumph Books, 1994.

Nash, Bruce, and Allan Zullo. *The Baseball Hall of Shame*. New York, NY: Pocket Books, 1985.

________, and ________. *The Baseball Hall of Shame 2*. New York: NY: Pocket Books, 1986.

Nemec, David, et al. *20th Century Baseball Chronicle*. Lincolnwood, IL: Publications International, 1993.

Okrent, Daniel, and Steve Wulf. *Baseball Anecdotes*. New York, NY: Harper & Row, 1989.

Reichler, Joseph L., ed. *The World Series: A 75th Anniversary*. New York, NY: Simon and Schuster, 1978.

Reidenbaugh, Lowell. *Cooperstown: Where the Legends Live Forever*. New York, NY: Arlington House, 1988.

Reston, James, Jr. *Collision at Home Plate*. New York, NY: Harper Collins, 1991.

Rose, Pete, and Roger Kahn. *Pete Rose: My Story*. New York: NY: Macmillan, 1989.

Rosenburg, John M. *They Gave Us Baseball*. Harrisburg, PA: Stackpole Books, 1989.

Rubin, Robert. *Ty Cobb: The Greatest*. New York, NY: G.P. Putnam's Sons, 1978.

Ruth, Babe. *The Babe Ruth Story*. New York, NY: Scholastic Book Services, 1948.

Shatzkin, Mike, ed. *The Ballplayers*. New York: NY: Arbor House, 1990.

Sobol, Ken. *Babe Ruth & the American Dream*. New York, NY: Random House, 1974.

Sokolove, Michael Y. *Hustle: The Myth, Life and Lies of Pete Rose*. New York, NY: Simon and Schuster, 1990.

Wagenheim, Kal. *Babe Ruth: His Life and Legend*. New York, NY: Henry Holt, 1974.

Wallop, Douglas. *Baseball: An Informal History*. New York, NY: Bantam, 1970.

Zoss, Joel, and John S. Bowman. *The American League*. New York, NY: Gallery Books, 1986.

_______, and _______. *The National League*. Hong Kong: Bison Books, 1986.

Index